ESCAPING the PROTECTORS

Based on a True-Life Story

BY SADE ENIOLA

ISBN: 978-1-915147-47-9 (Paperback)
ISBN: 978-1-915147-48-6 (Ebook)

Book Design by HMDpublishing

CONTENTS

INTRODUCTION

Nobody has a perfect life. Everyone has something they are dealing with in one way or the other. This book gives a first-hand perspective of what it looks like to grow up in a world where you don't have a support system. Although this is based on a true-life story, the names of the characters in the book are made up. The names have been modified to protect each character's identity. In addition, the places and schools mentioned are made up. Everything referenced in the story is based on personal knowledge and experience. This book is not intended for my readers to attack any person or any organizations, but to simply help educate about the effects of societal pressure, illuminate and educate readers about Nigerian cultures, and motivate and empower people from all walks of life, both young and old. This book highlights how some people in power take advantage of the helpless. Most importantly, I wrote this book to emphasize that abuse is not acceptable and to urge all readers to render help against such a despicable event when necessary.

Similar to Damilola's story, this book depicts the suffering of millions of children all around the world. At some point in our lives, we have all witnessed, seen, or heard stories of someone who was abused. Remember to always help those children who are in need and to speak up when you see something. You'll never know how amazing that help is and how much of a difference you're making in the lives of others. Children are the future. We want a better generation.

Writing this book was challenging, especially because it's based on a true-life story. In addition, this piece brought back some unfortunate and uneasy events to discuss, along with the main character having to relive the painful memories. On the other hand, this piece has moved me to be able to help others. An experience shared is an experience learned and I believe people will be able to learn one or two things from reading it and maybe it will inspire others to share their stories. Writing this piece encouraged the main character to open up. As she described it, the discussion helped her tremendously and it was better than seeing a therapist. Since sharing her story, she has learned to be more open, and she doesn't feel shamed by her past any longer.

I hope this book helps and encourages others who might be going through the same struggles. I want my readers to understand that societal pressure and peer influence affect one another. I also want parents to understand how their role plays a huge part in their children's lives. When we are born, the first set of people we learn to trust and rely on is our parents. As we watch these adults and see them as our heroes, their attitudes about life shape and influence us. Slowly but surely, we pick up these habits. My goal is to offer hope and to encourage anyone who might be going through the same dilemma to speak up.

Escaping the Protectors is based on the true-life story of a young Nigerian girl named Damilola (Dami) Adeleke who went through many struggles as a child. This book takes you through her journey: the emotional rollercoaster of what it feels like being poor and growing up in a Nigerian society that is filled with gender inequality and where wealth and religiosity trump everything. The main character described her internal struggle with her religious background while trying to win the love of her mother and prove her worth. One night, she stared into the dark blue peaceful sky and made a wish upon the stars. Her wish, many years later, seemed to come to pass when she discovered herself in a new world, although she had not realized it yet. Is it the end of her struggle or is it just the beginning? Do wishes really come true?

The story of Damilola is very motivational for both the young and old. Hopefully, most people will relate to her and learn one or two things from her personal life story. My goal is to inspire my readers about the power of not giving up and having hopes and dreams. Damilola [meaning "blessed with wealth" in Yoruba] dreams big. This storyline teaches the value of perseverance and willingness to be better. In life, self-perseverance and resiliency are the keys to achieving a greater height.

CHAPTER ONE:

ILARA-MOKIN, HOMETOWN

I grew up in a family of eight—a mom, dad, five siblings, and myself. Dad was an owner and a pastor in charge of a Christ Apostolic Church (CAC) in Ilara-Mokin (Ilara), a small local village in the central part of Ifedore local government Ondo State, Nigeria. Ilara is inside Akure[1]. The church was built near the stream. Next to the church is a bridge.

Once or twice, during a rainy season, the bridge overfilled, causing water to flow into the uncompleted, *doorless and windowless* church, destroying the church equipment and wooden benches. Five minutes' walk away from the church is our house, a small flat surrounded by a red gate with a spike thorn on top. The thorn kept out intruders and prevented burglars from climbing over the gate to rob the house. Gates are essential when it comes to living in Nigeria due to the high level of insecurity.

---

1   Akure - capital of Ondo State, city of southwest Nigeria.

As you enter our compound, you would see a well[2] or a borehole on the right. The well was where we fetched water for the house, and next to it were rope lines for spreading clothes when they were washed. The flat was divided into two sections, one to the right and one to the left. We lived on the left side while the right side was rented out to a tenant. The one thing I like about Nigeria is there is no such thing as a mortgage. When you build or buy a house, the house automatically belongs to you. No mortgage, no taxes. Everything is done upfront and out of pocket cost because it was a cash and carry system, not a credit rating system, you pay for what you can afford and if you can't afford it, you save until you can buy it. In Nigeria, no government officials can come and invade your privacy or tell you what to do; your property is your property. No need for a permit or license to upgrade or do anything at your house. Everyone makes their choice based on their discretion. In Nigeria, family triumphs over government officials' rules and regulations regarding ways of life and family decision. The head of the house, usually the father, makes up their own rules and regulations for their own household. The only exceptions are when it comes to renting. The landlords have the power to do whatever they feel fit. This is the only aspect that makes living in Nigeria easier. Bills are paid yearly rather than monthly with the exceptions of buying data for your phone usage or paying for your own power supplies that you rarely get. Although this makes Nigeria easier, it is also what makes the country corrupt.

---

2   Well - underground water, created by digging and drilling the ground to create water access. Due to lack of running water in most Africans' homes, wells are built in the compound to grants people access to water.

People feel they can do whatever they want without abiding by the few laws of the land; most especially the people in the echelons of power and wealth: governors, presidents, police officers, pastors, and traditional chiefs. These are the most corrupt of them all.

Anyway, my mom was a stay-at-home wife. The source of income was money coming from church members as gifts for the man of God. We also ate food we harvested from our farm. From this small income, eight of us ate. Each season could be brutal; sometimes, we had a lot to harvest, and other times, nothing at all. So, with six female children from one wife, it could be challenging to feed everyone. In addition, before my father converted into a Christian and became a pastor, he had also married two other wives from previous relationships, marrying and divorcing them one after the other and having kids with each one.

So, technically, I have seven siblings. I have one half-brother and one half-sister from other mothers. But in our household, it is just my mom Mary, my dad Samuel, and my five sisters (Ade, Esther, Tiwa, Bisola, and Debby). Whatever happened to those half-siblings, I have no idea. I suppose they are probably with their mothers, struggling without a father figure in their homes.

Unlike those in first world countries, fathers in Nigeria are not obligated to pay child support. If a husband were to abandon his wife and his kids, the woman has to start her life again. She would have to move out of the husband's house or be kicked out along with her children, who were now the woman's sole responsibility. Nigeria is a man-ruled society; a man's world. That is why you'll find men marrying multiple wives without consequences because those men feel entitled, only a good loving husband will cherish his woman and kids. Society has made some of these men feel like they can do whatever they want. The worst part is that the chance of the woman getting remarried is slim to none. "Who wants to marry you with all these kids," society would always say. Nobody ever wants to marry a single mother. And by a stroke of luck, if a woman were to remarry, she would be God-damn lucky if the new father-figure treated her kids as his own biological children. In some instances, when it comes to assistance and support from the in-laws on the husband's side, uncles, sisters, parents, and even grandparents can make matters worse for the women in the relationship. They will instead mock and help to throw the woman out of her home. These in-laws feel entitled and believe their son's or brother's homes also belong to them. The woman has no power, and neither do her parents. Sometimes, the wife or her parent might have to beg the in-laws to take the wife back.

It is the same for the single females who are suitable for marriage. Because nobody wants to marry a single mother, typically these men end up marrying young and beautiful ladies. If a single father loses his wife, and for some reason he gets to keep his kids, those children would also be considered lucky if the new stepmother treated them right. It's like the Cinderella story with the evil stepmom. But again, in this narrative, the mistreatment of the children is usually hidden without the man's knowledge. Once the man discovered the truth of how his woman had been treating his kids, it's a different ballgame. He can throw her out of the house, or she'd beg for a second chance to be a better person. The opposite can be said for the women. In an instance where single mothers end up remarrying, these women would turn blind eye to their children's suffering despite their knowledge of how the kids are being treated by the husband. Sometimes, these same women might even turn against their children due to not wanting to lose their new marriage. Both genders can be classified as evil when it comes to nurturing children that is not their biological blood. In the ends, both the children and the poor single mother struggle to survive. These are the realities, especially in middle and low-income families, or families where the majority of its members are illiterate.

Living in Nigeria can be tough, although I am sure other countries can be equally challenging. Since I only know Nigeria, I can only speak of my people. The only thing I do not understand is why low-income families tend to reproduce so many children when they know that there are not sufficient incomes to care for them all? They bring children into a world of suffering and poverty. The matter worsens when the husband passes, leaving the woman alone to suffer. Children begin begging for food so they can eat. Simple access to food and shelter is difficult. The only possible way is for children to drop out of school and parade themselves on the streets to assist their mothers. Some older children like the girls might join prostitution without the mother's knowledge, but in most cases, these children usually sell produce such as food, drinks, and snacks on the street in order to earn some cash. In other cases, the woman might give her children away so she can be relieved. People make fake promises stating they would help or care for their children, but only to treat the child as a housemaid. In other tribes, the poor family might send their children to trade in order for the child to help support their families.

Honestly, the difference between the rich and poor can be very distinguished. The rich would rather send their children to study abroad because quality education is considered better in western universities than any university degree obtained in Nigeria. The same goes for rich pregnant and laboring mothers, who give birth outside the country, rather than in the country. To live and survive in Nigeria requires money because money speaks. The rich continue to prosper while the poor remain poor and helpless. The corrupt politicians find ways to embezzle all the money for themselves and their families, instead of rebuilding the country. That's why if you travel to some parts of Lagos like Lekki, Ikoyi, and, or Abuja, you will find the majority of the wealthy people residing there. The roads are well paved with little to no potholes and with amazing infrastructure. As I was saying, this high-class mogul keeps the citizens and community poor. They build schools and hospitals that are unattainable and unaffordable to common citizens. If you do not have money, no one recognizes you. You are better off dead because money trumps everything.

During my parents' time, they believed children were blessings from God, but this was due to their lack of education as well as their cultural beliefs. They believe the more children you have, the greater the chances are that at least one of them will become something greater. As African parents always say, they want someone to take care of them in their old dying age. These parents place all pressure and all responsibility of caring for them onto their children. And by luck, if you become the breadwinner of the family, you would have to carry the burden of caring for everyone, including all the siblings. In addition, Mom and Dad just wanted to have a male child together, a man that would carry on the family name, so for this reason they kept trying. Moreover, they don't believe in the idea of contraception, a form of birth control. Nigerian older generations condemned the idea of females using birth control and anyone using one is viewed as wayward and a prostitute.

Having a male child in Nigerian communities is potent. Men rule the world, or as people say, it is a man's world. A male can carry the family's name while females' maiden names will be changed once they're married. It seems that women are just meant for childbearing and taking care of the home. Women are viewed as not able to hold a job once they start having children. The woman will have to stay home and care for her family because, like in most African countries that I know, people believe that a woman's place and responsibility is in the kitchen. The woman going on maternity leave poses a threat to the company because there is a hold on her position.

In most cases, especially in the non-educated areas, if a woman returns to work after giving birth, she might be deemed irresponsible by society, which believes she has abandoned her husband and home. Nigerian people care so much about society's opinion. The pressures from the community are too much. On the other hand, men are considered desirable, strong, and respectable. Men usually do not go on paternity leave. They carry their father's name.

They, the society, make it seem that once women are married, they no longer belong to their family. The tradition of bride price[3] seems like an idea of the female child being sold to her husband's family-to-be, although others might consider it as a day of celebration of the union of two families. A day full of lively afrobeat music, dancing, delicious delicacies, food entrées, and many people wearing colorful, authentic Nigerian fabrics. This is a day where you have many uninvited guests, who come just to eat, drink, and take food home in excess. Whether invited or not, these people come to join the party. But again, "bride price," why are women being sold to the men? Traditionally, if a man wants to marry a woman in Nigeria, he would travel to the girl's village to meet her parents and the village elders. Once approved, the girl's family along with the elders would now have to come up with a list of demands for the prospective husband-to-be. These lists of demands can be outrageous but demands vary from family to family. Some families might demand cars, two, three, or even up to four cows, goats, five bags of rice, yams, money, and so on. The list is never ending and there are no specified amounts of things being demanded. When a problem rises in the future within the union or in a case where there is domestic abuse, the bride's family cannot afford to pay back the list of demands. They would prefer their girl child to stay in the domestic abuse and tolerate her husband or the in-laws.

---

3   Bride price - Western Nigerian tradition of the groom's family buying items requested by the bride's family. List of demanded items consists of many foods, clothing materials, and large sum of money.

In most cases, they would advise her to continue praying because to the parent, God is the only person who can change the abuser and the circumstances. Although not all marriage ends in abuse, I believe this gives power of ownership over the bride. She is his property until the family is capable of paying back everything.

In an event where both the man and woman apply for a job, the man would be preferred for the job positions, despite the level of qualifications. When dealing with a poor social class, the family would rather send their male child to school than a female. In most marital homes, the men would prefer their wives to be stay-at-home wives while bringing in the money because they are the provider. I believe this gives the power of dominion over the woman and serves as a disadvantage because she is classified as just a woman. In addition, women who are suitable for marriage tend to reside with their parents until the right man comes to marry them off. At this point, that is when you would see her leave her parent and move to her husband's house. This creates a disparity between the two genders. It not only allowed women to be dependent solely on their husbands, but it also placed a great burden and pressure on young men. This is the complete opposite when it comes to living in the western world. In a social gathering, women are not allowed to talk among men. This idea though varies from tribe to tribe.

But this all came to an end when Dad passed away. No more attempting to have a male child. Dad was gone, and that was it. And there was Mom — a widow at thirty-three years old. Now, the only source of food was the farm and whatever it could produce. The little money coming from the church also ceased when Dad passed away. Because Mom was a woman, the church was taken over by another male preacher. Every two to three years, male preachers were rotated through our church. Again, in the Nigerian community, during my parents' time, women preaching on the Altar of God was considered an abomination. She could still be the church's deaconess out of respect for her late husband but was never allowed to preach.

Months after I turned four, right before Dad's passing, he became sick. How he got sick, I do not know. He was a healthy man, hardworking, and dedicated all his life to church and God. I understand that sometimes, people just fall ill, but that shouldn't lead to death. And in the case of illness, proper medical treatment should be sought. But in Nigeria, people place religion over everything. On one street, you'll see about four to five different churches surrounding that one street. I am not joking, and this is not an exaggeration. In Nigeria, there are more churches than any business. In today's generation, only the quick-witted mind views and sees that some of these churches are more of a business, owned by fake prophets who are proclaiming to be men of God. The sad truth, many of the poor don't seem to get this idea. They are blind because they all want to make it to Heaven. To the poor and the non-educated, any man who carries the Bible and speaks at the altar of God is a man of God. They believe he must be speaking the truth, not caring to read their own Bible and see for themselves what is written. So, for this reason, they put all their little to no income in the church's offering basket for God and the man of God to bless them. You would see these pastors driving nice cars, wearing the best clothes, and living in nice houses, while their church members can't afford one square meal.

Due to a lack of education, poverty, and ridiculous religious beliefs, proper medical care could not be obtained. Too much religiosity and tribalism. Don't take this wrong, I love God and believe in Jesus Christ; but I believe there are times when medical treatments are necessary and trump religion. As a matter of fact, I believe coupling religion and medical help are effective in healing. Spirituality gives hope for a better outcome and that God is by your side. But in Nigeria, people will prefer God to handle their sickness because God is a miracle healer, who raises the dead and heals the blind.

As a pastor's child, I remember the daily morning devotions, praying, and after-church practices. Dad spent most of his time in church, proclaiming the name of God into peoples' life. Out of seven days in a week, dad spent one hundred percent of his time in church doing God's work. The church was our life. We spent so much time in church that mom ended up giving birth to me inside the church. Today, I can say that I am a product of the Christ Apostolic church, born on January 2nd, 1994, right after a church program. Mom was waiting for Dad so that they could head home together after the service. Most of the members had gone home, and the only people left were the church ministers in the back room having their meetings. Behold, Mom went into labor and delivered me right there in the center of the church. As she explained it, she untied her Ankara[4] wrapped around her waist, spread it on the ground, and had to deliver me all on her own. She yelled, and the old lady that lives near the church came to help her cut the baby's umbilical cord. She wrapped me up in the Ankara and took me home. She prayed over me and laid me to sleep. As she described it, she never had to take me to the hospital, and I was fine. Up to now at my current age, as I am telling this story, I have never been hospitalized for anything. I am in good health, and I thank God for my life.

So, in the end, I cannot say I have distaste for church or God. I love God, and I believe in Jesus. I do not understand why Nigeria is so religious but the people are so evil at the same time. I guess that's why the Bible says, "The hearts of men are wicked." But I will say that if we love God and serve him diligently, then why does he allow bad things to happen to his people and children? I love God, but like almost everyone, my faith is often shaken. What is the purpose of life?

I only wish I could recall memories of my dad. I always wonder how things would have been if Dad was still alive. How would my life be today? I guess that will always be the "What if" moment.

____

4   Ankara - African fabric made of multiple unique colors

CHAPTER TWO:

WHERE IT ALL BEGINS

This is where my life journey began; at least, this is where I could remember it. It all started twenty-one years ago, after turning four years old, I noticed Dad was no longer seen at the house. Well, he was hardly seen in the house in the first place. Later, I learned he wasn't feeling well. Mom was all that was left. With Dad not being there, we had nothing else except the little food from the farm. Just Mom and six children, with no job or source of income. The struggle became real. Mom opened a small shop in front of the house to make money. We sold foodstuffs such as raw rice, red beans, garri[5], and elubo[6]. Sometimes, my sisters and I walked around the street carrying baskets of food and drinks on our heads to sell to the public. This helped us generate some income.

---

5   Garri – Western Africa dish made of processed cassava

6   Elubo - yam flour; yam cut into small pieces, fried, and then ground into smooth brown flour

A few months later, I didn't know how it happened, but I was suddenly living with a strange single woman. They said she was a doctor, but I knew nothing of this lady doctor. I didn't even know her name. One day, she came to my village and picked me up, and the rest is history. That was where my life journey began. Never did I see my sisters and mom again. That was how I got separated from my family and began living with brutal Nigerian families.

We arrived at this lady's house on a cold, gloomy night. The house was dark and dreary. The moment I got to the house, she dragged me and pushed me into a dark room, and then she left. Behind me was a mirror mounted to the wall. I turned around and looked into the mirror, and I began to cry. I felt a cold shiver run down my body. The lady doctor came back and threw an Ankara at me. I spread the cloth on the ground and made it my bed. Then the 'lady doctor' went to her cushion comfy bed. I lay on the cold hard ground throughout the night, sobbing my eyes out.

"So, this is how life is? Dad is sick and nowhere to be found, and suddenly Mom shipped me off to a different family," I murmured all through the night. I continued to cry until I fell asleep. At 5 A.M. the next morning, I was awakened by a cold hard slap on my back. I was so confused because I didn't know what hit me. I shouted and began to cry.

"Get up! Get up! There is a lot to be done today," the lady doctor said. "You have the entire house that needs to be cleaned and the compound that needs to be swept. Hurry up! Those places won't clean themselves. Then after, when you are done, wake me up so we can go cook in the kitchen."

I looked into the wall mirror once again. My face was swollen from my tears. I began to cry once more. *Where did Dad go, and where is Mom? Why are all these things happening to me? God, what have I done to deserve the cruel punishment?* These were the questions running through my mind while I continued to cry. At the same time, I prayed to God to change my situation or wake me up from this nightmare.

At 6 A.M., I was in the kitchen when I heard the lady doctor's footsteps. I suppose she was going to the bathroom because it was not yet time to wake her up. At the sound of her footsteps, a cold shiver ran down my spine, my heart pumping and beating so fast that it felt like it would pop out of my chest. I rushed to finish cleaning the house and ran outside to sweep the compound. I have to get this done, oh my god. I started to cry. About thirty minutes later, I was done cleaning. I ran inside, and I looked at the time on the wall clock in the hallway, it was five minutes to seven. I ran to her brown bedroom doorway to wait for the next task. As she opened the door, I quickly turned my head and looked down at her foot. In Nigerian culture, looking at an elder or someone older than you straight in the eyes is considered disrespectful.

"Great! You are done." She walked around the house. "You did okay. Now, let's go make food. Do you know how to cook?"

Considering that I was only four years old, she should have known I couldn't make anything. How could I possibly cook? "No ma'am," I replied.

"Well, starting today, you will learn," she stated. "When I am cooking, you'll be there, watching."

"Okay, ma'am," I replied.

"Good. Now, let's go to the market. I'll show you around the place."

"Yes, ma'am."

The next six months I spent living with the woman seemed like I was cast in a horror movie. Every day was a challenge of its own. *God, why have you abandoned me?* I always wondered. I always desired to leave the house. I couldn't continue that way. Every day was another day of being beaten, slapped, and starved. Sometimes, I went days without eating. Other times, the neighbor would see me and quickly offer me meals before she arrived back home.

One Saturday morning, at 6 A.M., she ordered me to pick up all the animals' feces on the street. "Every morning, before the sunrise, you need to go pick all the animals' poop; mix it in a bucket, and used it to fertilize the farm," she said.

Nigeria is a place where animals such as cows, goats, chickens, etc. roam the streets. If you wake up early enough at a local time, you'll see animals' feces all over the streets and towns. As instructed, on Saturday early morning, I walked around, picking up cows and goat feces with my bare hand. That morning, my task was to pick and mix all the feces into a huge bucket, head to the garden near the house, sprinkle the mixture, and use it as a fertilizer. Picking animal feces with my bare hand was disgusting, but after a while, I got used to it.

After seven months of this cold brutality, I could not take it anymore. The only cloth I had was the same native mixture of brown and blue printed Ankara dress that I had worn to the house. By then, the dress was torn on the arms, middle section, and bottom. I had to leave that place. *Dami? Think: what is the plan for you to get out of here?* I thought to myself.

One breezy midnight, when the lady doctor was asleep, I tiptoed through the long hallway and left. I was free. I don't know how, but I was heading back to my village. I left the house and closed the door behind me. I had attempted to run away before but had stopped when I opened the front door and saw a faceless woman, dressed in a white garment. I had stood at the door silently, watching. In one hand was a bell and in the other, a Bible. I was so scared that I ran back inside the house. But tonight was different. No freaky lady wandering in the middle of the night.

At first, running away was nerve-wracking, but then I summoned up the courage and wasn't scared anymore. The fear disappeared. I walked barefooted through the towns. The night was cold and windy. Different animal sounds came from the woods. Crickets chirped, and owls hooted. Throughout the night, I stopped multiple times, passing the night in the bush. I walked as far as I could until I could not walk anymore. I fell asleep, woke, and continued walking. By late morning, I made it back to Ilara. My mom was surprised to see me. She looked at me in dismay.

"What are you doing here? Where is Dr. Adegero?" I said nothing. She had an infuriated, disappointed, but at the same time, a sad expression on her face. "Okay. Get inside!" she said in Yoruba[7].

I went inside the house to meet my sisters. Nobody said a word. They all looked at me. I walked quietly and timidly inside the living room and took a seat. All I could think of was how unhappy mom looked with that angry voice. I sat in one of the torn chairs and began to cry. At the same time, I couldn't help but think, so that was the woman's name, Dr. Mrs. Adegero. I didn't even know she was married. I had lived with this woman for seven months; never once did I see any man come into the house. Where were her husband and children anyway? Did the husband die? Oh well, at least, I was out of there. But again, did I make the right choice of running away? Mom was not even happy to see me. She looked very disappointed in me.

That's how it was, until two weeks later. My mom and I drove to a town to meet a couple. Mom was dressed in her native wear and gele[8]. We got to a church and later went into the couples' house. Sitting in their living room, I overheard the pastor and his wife talking to Mom. Towards the evening as the night was approaching, my mom pulled me to the side and said, "These people are

---

7   Yoruba - one of many spoken languages in Nigeria
8   Gele - Nigerian head tie/wrap

your father's friends, and they have come to help me. You will be staying with them. They are nice people."

My heart started to break, and I started to cry. Soon, I watched my mom get into a yellow and blue taxicab. Then, off she went. I cried for the rest of the night. Although I was sad, the night was not bad. There was also an older girl, probably in her teens. I assume she was a maid based on how she looked. Skinny and tall with a fair complexion. She said her name was Tope. The pastor and the wife had three kids: one boy and two girls. Living inside the house was the grandfather, the pastor, his wife, and three children. The grandfather was also a pastor. They lived in a second-floor apartment with blue painted walls. Next to the apartment was their church.

The church window was made of beautiful glass. It looked like a Catholic church, but it was not. Mom was not Catholic, and she would never allow a Catholic believer to take her daughter. As I said before, Nigeria and its societies are too tribalistic, religious, and also very judgmental of other believers because they have different practices, views, and ideologies of God and Jesus.

I suppose that church was probably the Anglican Church. Every service was full—nice wooden benches with the Bible behind every bench. The surprising thing: I never saw the pastor preach, not since I had been there anyway. Instead, I watched the grandfather sit among the ministers up on stage, wearing his long white robe.

Living in the pastor's house was not bad. Tope and I both slept on the living room floor. We laid our clothes on the ground, and that was our bed. I was quite used to this now. Still being maltreated but I think Tope got the most beatings because she was older. We didn't get along, but we worked together and split tasks. She did most of the heavy lifting and daunting jobs. Most times, she cooked, and I helped. Other times, the pastor's wife cooked. One night, while everyone was sleeping, I heard small soft footsteps making its way to the living room where Tope and I were sleeping. I covered my head with Ankara, pretending to be asleep, and began peeping through the see-through cloth. It was the grandfather tiptoeing towards us.

In his hand was his lantern. Most times in Nigeria, there is no electricity or power supply. We use lanterns, flashlights, and candles as light sources to help us see in the dark, most notably at night. Only the wealthy and middle-class people might be able to afford generators. I noted the grandfather continued to walk up and down, then slowly. He approached Tope. He waved the lantern around, shining a light on each of us to check if we are sleeping. I closed my eyes in fear, then opened them again. He then placed the lantern down. I watched him lift Tope's skirt and then pulled down his white undergarment. I was shocked and didn't know what was happening. I held my breath, and minutes later, he was done. The grandfather pulled up his underwear, picked the lantern up, and walked away into the dark. I was in disbelief, but again, I didn't know what was happening. Deep down, I felt like he was hurting Tope, but Tope never made a sound, she just laid there; quiet and still.

In the morning, I looked at Tope and tried to ask her if she was okay. She pushed my shoulder, snapped, and then walked away. Why was she so upset, I thought? One month later, Tope was gone. I didn't see her anymore. I was getting pretty used to her, but now she was gone, and I was alone. After Tope left, I began doing all the house chores. I cleaned, cooked, and got the pastor's kids ready for school. While they were in school, I continued with the house chores, handwashing all the dirty clothes.

One and a half months later, my mom showed up. She looked distraught. She pulled my hand and said we were leaving. I was kind of happy to see her but not really. I didn't feel anything for her. I was in an emotionless state of mind. The main thing that caught my attention was she said we are leaving. I guess I was done living with these couples. I wonder what happened between them. Mom coming to pick me up randomly was unusual. Something happened. Possibly a fight or disagreements must have occurred between my mom and the pastor's wife or something along that area. We entered the taxi cab, and I looked back at the old, painted blue apartment. I couldn't help but smile on the inside. I was not going to miss this place.

CHAPTER THREE

GIRL IN PROGRESS

It was a long quiet ride back home. I was quiet. Mom was seated in the passenger seat while I was sitting in the back. We got home later in the evening. I went inside and joined the rest of my sisters. Auntie Ade had made some rice and stew. After we finished eating, we all prayed and went to bed. Two days after, while sitting on the porch, Mom came outside. She informed me that I would be going back to Doctor Missus Adegero's house.

Oh my God, why is it always me? Why do I have to go? I thought to myself. I had just come back from one person's house, and it had been a few days, and behold once again; she was sending me off. In Nigerian cultures and traditions, arguing with one's parent or anyone older is unacceptable. You can get smacked because they believe in discipline. Everyone must show respect to their elders, even if they are just a year older. Only in Nigerian culture respect is not earned; most adults feel it's their due diligence to get respect for the sake of being older.

Whether related or not, everyone is an Auntie or uncle, sister or brother, or sir or ma'am as long as the person is older. You must respect them at all costs, and most of all, there is no such thing as arguing or talking back. Nigerian adults find it difficult to apologize to someone their junior even if they are at fault, and when they are wrong, they will never admit to their mistakes. This idea of silencing children creates a lack of creativity, critical thinking, and self-expression. As a child, you cannot ask why, your job is to follow orders. These adults believe children's opinion doesn't matter.

"While you were gone, she came here," Mom said. Was this the reason why she came to pick me up, because Dr. Adegero came looking for me? I was gone for five months, living with the pastor and his wife and suddenly she decided to come to the house to look for me. Strangely, Mom agreed. Mom continued to talk, and I just listened. I didn't utter a word. Finally, I got the courage to tell her, "I don't want to go back." She said nothing.

Days later, I was back in Dr. Adegero's house. This time, there was a boy older than me living in the house. His name was Wale. Wale was about twelve to thirteen years old. Slender and fair in complexion. Also, there was a single mother with a baby girl renting one of the rooms. Coming into her house, I already knew what to expect. Every day was similar to before—the same beatings and starvation for days without food or little food. When the lady stepped out, I spent time with the tailor in front of her house. I watched her sew clothes. Before the *witch* came back, I made sure the house was in tip-top shape. Wale's job was to go work on the farm across from the house and clean the compound, while my job remained taking care of the entire house, handwashing all the clothes, and assisting Wale on the farm.

The lady and I continued to cook together. When food was ready, she made me serve it and wait on her. Often times, she would go to the living room or her bedroom. Then, I had to serve the food on a plate and take it to her. She made me stand and watch her eat. Sometimes, while serving her, I would spit in her meals. Then, I would stand and watch her eat. I became an angry little girl. Part of me was angry, but at the same time I felt terrible for my actions. I think she deserved more than spit in her food, but at the same time, I couldn't help feeling guilty. I noticed she tended to treat Wale better.

One Friday afternoon, when I was outside on the porch, she walked up to me and asked who stole the meat from the stove's pot of stew. As always, before I could say I didn't do it, a slap landed on my face. I began to cry. Maybe God was punishing me for my actions. I informed her I didn't do it.

"Lie!" She yelled as she made me kneel on the ground and hold my arms up in the air.

"I swear to God, I didn't do it," I replied.

"Lying in the name of God?" She asked. "Until you tell me who did it, you will be there!" She stepped out of the house and left me. About four hours later, she returned. In her hand was a long cane. "Are you ready to tell the truth?"

"I, I, I, I didn't do it!" I stuttered.

She whipped me with the cane while saying a child of God doesn't lie or steal. She kicked me to the ground and continued to flog me with a cane until I couldn't cry anymore.

"That's your food for the night." She left me outside and went in and locked the door.

In the middle of the night, her tenant tiptoed outside. I looked at her and she placed her pointer finger over her lips, signaling for me to hush. She took me inside to her bedroom and locked her door. As I sat on her bedroom floor, I looked at the baby on the small mattress. The baby was asleep. She offered me some rice and stew. After finishing eating the delicious meal, she advised me not to inform anyone. "Go to sleep," she said. In the early morning at 4:30, she woke me up and took me back outside. I laid back in the same position until dawn.

At 6 A.M., Dr. Adegero came outside and hissed at me. I got up, and went inside to begin my morning chores. As I went inside, I looked at the wall mirror, my body bruised with cane marks. It hurt so badly. My face was swollen. *God, why don't you just kill me? Kill me and take me away. Besides, where is Dad? What happened to Dad? I am tired of this world, and I don't want to be here anymore.* I was deep in thought when I heard footsteps. I came out of the door and went to the kitchen to pick up the broom. I began the daily chores, cleaning, and starting with her room first, then worked my way down to the kitchen. Cleaning the house, I couldn't help but cry. Tears won't stop pouring even when I tried to stop.

Those days, she accused me of stealing meats from the pot. If it was not meat, it was her items or money. She didn't even bother to ask Wale. She just assumed everything was me and went off like a wild animal, beating and stomping on me. I used to live in that house, and nothing had ever gone missing. Now, this Wale guy was here, and things were vanishing into thin air. Never once did I see her question him. I guess it was probably because I handled the inside the house, but it still doesn't make sense.

At least three times a month, she would accuse me of stealing meat and food from the pot. Although I knew I didn't do it, it was something I learned to deal with. While she punished me, she would keep repeating, "You will never learn." Most nights, I went to bed crying.

"Dad, wherever you are, I miss you. Please, Dad, come home soon."

One random day, my mom showed up in a taxi parked on the roadside near the house. Did she come to pick me up or just visit? It was strange, and that didn't sound like her. She had never once visited or called. So, something must have happened. Moments later, the taxi driver came down from the car, came inside the house, held my hand, and told me to get in the car. As we approached the car, I wasn't happy to see Mom, but I was glad to be leaving that hell hole.

As I stepped inside, Dad was in the back seat, strapped with a seatbelt. Mom was sitting in the passenger seat and screaming at the top of her voice in despair. I tried to look at Dad's eyes. He was wearing dark sunglasses. I could hardly see his eyes. He had on a white suit and a pair of black trouser pants on. I tapped him on his left thigh as I was sitting to his left. He didn't even budge or pay attention to me. I shook his left leg vigorously but with no response. Then I stopped trying to get his attention. Why was Mom crying, anyway? What's going on here? I leaned next to Dad in silence and rested my head on his arm until we got back to our village.

As we got to the house, I went inside to change my ragged clothes into a clean native dress. The house was filled with people. Mom continued to cry her eyes out. Dad was taken to his room by three strange men. The men plugged his nose and ears with cotton wool and covered him with a white garment sheet of cloth. Later, they brought in a large brown wooden coffin and took it into his room.

As nightfall approached, I began to grow weaker. By morning, I was sick. I laid in bed shaking. My whole body was covered with huge lumps that were extremely itchy. Later, I began to run a temperature with headaches and fever. My head hurt badly. For the next four days. I was not myself. I was very ill. Everyone was crying up and down, including myself.

On the third day, many people were at the house. Different families; mothers, fathers, children, and neighbors. I never even knew we had that many people. Everyone was wearing black native attire. The men dug a hole in the pavement of the house. Hours later, Mom came outside in black native attire. She was crying, and so was I. One of the older men picked me up and carried me in his arms. Four men came out of the house, carrying the coffin and then lowering it into the dug-up hole. I watched Mom grab some sand and toss it onto the coffin, followed by my sisters. I struggled to pick up the sand and toss it on the coffin as I followed their lead.

A few moments later, Dad was buried. There was a little celebration with music and some food as we didn't have much. After the burial party, people left and went their way. In Nigerian culture, there is always a burial celebration for the elderly after passing. Usually, on day of burial, people would wear black clothing, and years later, if funds are available, a huge party would be thrown in remembrance of the dead with vibrant colorful Nigerian fabric, foods, and lively afrobeat music. Although Dad wasn't old, he was older than Mom, so a small gathering was held. Vice versa occurs when it comes to children and younger persons passing unexpectedly. A small burial would be held, but it's mostly handled by someone else, usually the oldest sibling, aunties, or the grandma, but never the parent. It's a taboo for parents to handle the burial or watch their child laid to rest, this is a common practice, most especially in the Yoruba tribe. After the little gathering to celebrate him, days later, many people came to the house to mourn and greet Mom. Then, they went their way. Days after the burial, Mom continued to wear black clothing around the house. She shaved her head after Dad's death. (Some Nigerian cultures require the woman to shave their head after the death of their husband.) She was the new widow in town, a single woman with six female children. Many people thought we are not going to make it. Many thought we were all going to get pregnant since there was no father figure in the house. Many people thought of so many negative and evil things against us. The villagers we thought were our supporters were all condemning us. Adeleke's household was just females living in a country where women are considered powerless and are meant to be silent in men's presence.

CHAPTER FOUR

A NEW LIFE OF MINE

The next few days were a struggle. Mom struggled to feed us while she continued weeping. Fifteen days after Dad had been laid to rest, a couple named the Babalola came to our house. I was sitting outside on the porch, where Dad was buried, staring at his grave. Ade was inside the house, along with my other sisters. They entered the house, talked to mom, and left.

Since Dad had passed, Mom could not do anything. Our tradition forbids her from touching a knife or any sharp object. She also had to shave her hair and wear black clothing for the next six months. This practice was very hard. Most times, Auntie Ade had to help Mom in prepping meals and caring for us.

One month later, at the end of May, Mom told me to get ready. I packed one of my dresses, underwear, and a toothbrush. In the early morning, we left for Babalola's house. They lived in Oke-aro Idonre Garage in Akure,

Ondo State, Nigeria. After a one-hour taxicab ride, we finally arrived at the Babalola's house.

"There is no running away from this place. You are going to stay. Do you understand? And remember the daughter of whom you are," Mom added.

I nodded. Oh! I wished Dad was alive. Why did it always have to be me? I had other sisters, older sisters, as a matter of fact. But I was the one who was always given up. I was tired of going from home to home, and all the maltreatment. I looked at the house, my heart became heavy, and tear drops began rolling down my face.

Mr. and Mrs. Babalola's house looked like an apartment complex, but they claimed they owned the entire complex. They were renting the house to tenants, and it was the biggest house I had ever seen. The complex's exterior was painted with yellow and maroon colors while the interior walls were painted blue. Why would anyone use blue to paint the internal part of their home? Such an ugly color decision, I would say. But hey! What do I know?

The Babalola family lived upstairs in the first building. When we arrived at the house, Mom returned to Ilara. The same day, I met an older lady of an age suitable for marriage. She called herself Lola and introduced herself as one of the daughters. Then she introduced me to Kemi—a baby; I think about seven months old. I think Kemi was her daughter, but again, who was I to ask?

As the day passed, she showed me around the house and bedroom. The apartment was composed of three bedrooms, a living room connecting to the dining room, and one bathroom. To the back was the bathroom, where one side was a place for a shower, and the other side was the toilet. Also, in the back was the kitchen, a pantry for food storage, and an extra bedroom. The back door led to the backstairs to an atrium. In the atrium, there was a well and an open fire stove. The open fire method uses firewood for cooking. The atrium was also where the neighbors in the apartment complex fetched water for different reasons. The tradition of open fire stoves fueled by firewood is common among middle-class and low-income homes. The tenants shared the common space for cooking and spreading their hand washed clothes on the rope line.

This was my new home. Later in the day, I saw the man who had come to my house to see my Mom. Lola had finished cooking on the firewood outside in the atrium. We took the cooked food upstairs to the kitchen. I inevitably called her Auntie Lola as our culture demanded. While Lola worked in the kitchen, she told me her mom traveled, and she should be returning in a month.

"Yes, ma," I said.

She summoned me to go serve her dad. I placed the food on a tray and took it to the dining table that was set up. The moment I finished serving the food, her dad came out. I went to the kitchen and waited for the next instruction. After everyone was done eating, I went back to the table to clean up the table and wash the dishes.

On the last day of June, Mrs. Babalola showed up. As she arrived, I hurried out to collect her bag and took it upstairs. Months later, I noticed Auntie Lola was barely around, and actually, I didn't even see her in the house. Where could she have been or gone? A week passed without seeing Auntie Lola. I missed her. She was nice. She was the one person who had ever been nice to me. I thought I was going to like this place; it wasn't bad. I was not taking care of everything all by myself. Every morning, I helped her prep Kemi for daycare. Then, when we got back, we cleaned the house together. Best of all, she had never hit me.

CHAPTER FIVE

HERE WE GO AGAIN

I think I jinxed myself. I knew it was too good to be true. Unfortunately, a few weeks after Mrs. Babalola arrived, the drama started again. On the very first day of her return, Mr. and Mrs. Babalola were sitting in the living room, and I was in the dining when I overheard them saying they wanted my oldest sister, Ade. So why did Ade refuse to go? Why did Mom allow them to take me instead of her? Then, I heard them saying Ade refused, but instead, she convinced Mom that Mr. Babalola should take me. I could not believe my ears. *Does Mom hate me? Does Ade hate me? Is there something I do not know? Is there something about me and how many times have both Mom and Ade been doing this: refusing to give up Ade and my other sisters but intentionally giving me up each time?*

"She is too young and small, what can this tiny thing do?" Mrs. Babalola said.

Mrs. Babalola was what you call the real witch: Wicked Witch of the West, I'd say. She often looked at me with a cold brutal eye, like I had committed an unforgivable criminal act. After the second week, all hell broke loose. She made me do all the work in the house. Every morning at 5 A.M. she went to morning Mass. The Babalolas' were Catholic. I was surprised Mom was even allowing me to live with a Catholic family. Usually, Nigerian society frowned upon this—too much religiosity. Catholics, Muslims, and Christians couldn't even attend each other's events. Only on a few occasions, at least in the developed area, would you see these groups of individuals socializing. The societies' views of Christianity were somewhat different. Some parents will not allow their children to marry outside their religious practice or tribe. But I guess, in this case, Mom didn't care.

Before Mrs. Babalola's morning Mass, I had to be up by 4 A.M. Sleeping past four in the morning would be a wake-up call with cold water being dumped on me or a hand slap. In the first few weeks of her return, I often got the cold water. Soaked and drenched, I rolled up the thin hay mat where I had slept and spread it outside to dry. With all the mistreatments, the husband never said anything. He just watched it happen.

One morning, Mrs. Babalola was in the bathroom having her bath. She had finished bathing when she dropped her bar soap inside the toilet. She called me to pick it up. The toilet was full of stool. Without gloves, she forced me to pick up the soap. Trying to hold my breath, I reached into the toilet, pushed the stools to one side, and picked up her bar of soap. I cleansed it with the little remaining water in the bucket and placed it in her soap dish. She stood over me and watched the entire process.

It was like she enjoyed the act. I knew I should be used to this by now, but I couldn't help it. I have done this several times which includes, picking up animals' feces around the town, washing Kemi's stooling cloth napkins that serve as diapers, and washing the Babalola's occasional stool-stained underwear. I don't understand how they get stool to stick to their underwear despite using water to cleanse. I have to say that Mrs. Babalola is worse than her husband. Using water to cleanse the private part is a normal thing in Nigeria. Among the poor, people prefer water to use in the toilet rather than tissues because it is what they can afford. Toilet rolls are additional expenses and a luxury while water is available in excess and it does the same job. Also, they believe water cleanses better. But I guess in the case of the Babalolas', that theory doesn't matter. So, I should be used to this. The worst part, she never flushed the toilet, she leaves it for me to come and do it after she has done showering or after she leaves the bathroom.

Every day was the same. I woke up by four in the morning, fetched water from the well, and filled the entire house with water, including kitchens and all the bathroom's buckets. Once everyone was done showering, I continued to refill the household water, going up and down the stairs. I learned that fetching water in the early morning was the best time of the day. This allowed you to get the cleanest water for the house. If you wait until the sun is up, by that time many of the tenants must have fetched the clean water, leaving you with the worst part. The water left would be muddy and dirty, which no one could cook or shower with. Back then, most average homes in Nigeria didn't have running tap water. Some of the houses don't even have built-in faucets. Water coming from wells is fetched and used to cook, boiled for drinking if one cannot afford bottled or sachets-water[9].

Daily, I was Kemi's caretaker. I bathed, cleaned, fed, and even prepped her food for daycare. Once I dropped her off, I'd continue to do the house chores. I spent the entire day cleaning the house, washing everyone's clothes, and feeding the chickens. After breakfast, which was the only meal prepared in the kitchen, the rest of the cooking was done in the backyard, outside on the firewood. At noon, I would have to pick Kemi up from school. When we returned, the only way to get the rest of my tasks done was to place her on my back using a handwoven Ankara cloth. I'd tie it around my waist, which allowed her to sit snuggly against my back and her legs wrapped around my waist. This allowed my hands to be free and enabled me to continue the rest of my job. The sad part was that sometimes, Kemi would fall because the knot became loose. Before I could adjust the wrapper, Kemi was on the ground, screaming at top of her lungs. The moment Mrs. Babalola heard Kemi's crying, she would call my name, screaming and cursing at me with all kinds of profane words and names. I'd wipe my tears, pick Kemi and rock her back to sleep or until she stopped crying.

Living with the Babalolas was hell. In the beginning, I cried in bed every day, but after a while, I knew things were not going to change miraculously. I thought of running away multiple times, like the way I did at Dr. Adegero's house. Mom had instructed me to remain here. So,

---

9   Sachet-water - cleaned water sold in plastic bag

I had no place to go at all. If I were to run away and go back home, I figured Mom and Ade would be quick to ship me to a different house of a different family. On top of it all, it was not like any of the people I ever lived with treated me like a person. To these people, we were nobody but a piece of trash. They would be happy to take you in, maltreat you, and turn you into their maid. When you live with people in Africa, this is just an expectation. An expectation of maltreatment is because the family is not your biological parents. The odd part is the people that mistreat the child the most are usually jealous relatives: aunties, uncles, and friends. These are the people who you think would support you and have your back, but in the end, they show their true color of betrayal.

At the end of the night, I laid in bed thinking of God. I never ceased thinking that once I died, all the afflictions will be over. Maybe finally, I could join Dad in heaven because that day would be the best day ever. I knew it would. When Jesus left the earth, his persecution stopped and He finally went to join his father in Heaven. So, I prayed every night to God to take me away. But, until then, every day was the same.

CHAPTER SIX

ALL WILL BE WELL

It had been over six months since I had seen or heard from my mom. One random day, she came over to visit. I was delighted to see her but at the same time, surprised. I must admit that I looked ragged. I had no shoes. The only pair of slippers that I had brought with me had been broken a while back. I spent most of my time walking barefooted everywhere I went, whether to the market or to pick Kemi up from school. Sometimes, rusted nails pierced my foot and when this happened, I just pulled it out. Even though it was painful, I learned not to pay attention to it. My heels were as hard as wood and cracked open. Sometimes it hurt, but as time elapsed, I got used to the pain of the wound.

Mom looked at me but didn't say anything. I greeted her, and before she could answer, the wicked witch started to call. "Iya Ade!" Mrs. Babalola shouted. Iya means mother in the Yoruba language; Ade's mother. In our culture, societies usually call parents by their first child's name. The moment Mom got upstairs, she knelt and greeted them. I went straight into the kitchen to hide my face, anything to prevent them from noticing me. Just like how they maltreated me, Mom got the same treatment. I watched them send her everywhere, including the market, to buy groceries for the house.

"My husband and I want to eat fresh vegetable soup and some pounded yams. Here is some money. Go to the market and buy the ingredients needed. Hurry up!" said Mrs. Babalola.

"Yes, ma," Mom replied. It was sad watching my mother being humiliated, and the worst part was I couldn't do anything about it. I watched Mom trek in the hot blazing sun, heading to the food market around the house. She bought raw yams and fresh leafy vegetables, seasonings, dried and smoked fish, assorted meat, and *iru*[10]. While Mom cooked, I helped in prepping the soup. Mom chopped the veggies and I rinsed them with water. This was the only moment we had to spend together. She boiled yams until they were fully cooked, then, using a large wooden mortar and pestle, she pounded the yams until they became soft. Soft and doughy enough to be molded into a dough shape. Many foreigners know it as *Fufu*, but it's not. *Fufu* is made of cassava roots while pounded yam is made of yam roots, but they are both formed into the white dough at the end. Mom made vegetable soup- *efo-riro*[11].

---

10   Iru - locust beans; condiments
11   Efo-riro - local Nigerian soup dish made of green leafy vegetables - similar to spinach. Contains many assorted meats and spices

Before the meal could be done, Mrs. Babalola started insulting my mom and cursing at her.

"You are too slow! My husband and I are starving. When will the food be done?" When we finished, Mom hastened me to serve them their dish. The moment the food was done, Mom picked up her purse and headed back to Ilara. The sad part was that we did not get a chance to eat.

Once in a blue moon, Mom would visit. The few times Mom came over, they treated her like she was not a human. What do you expect from a wealthy family who thinks they are better than everyone else? Besides, since they were maltreating me, I was not surprised at the way they maltreated Mom. She was, after *all*, a helpless widow. The few times she came visiting, they sent her on errands, made her cook, clean, or even hand wash their clothes. Mom said nothing. She just did as she was told. Each time, the family demanded proper meals. At times, it was okra or *egusi* soup[12], which was made of melon seeds and leafy green vegetables. Other times, it was *efo-riro*, jollof rice[13], or fried rice. Most of the time, it was usually pounded yam. Mom made the best pounded yam and Ilara is known for its pounded yam and vegetable soup delicacies. Despite all the meal prepping, the only food I get to eat was their remains on their plates; their trash and bones. I'd clean up the dining and scrape the remains into a bowl. This was my meal; lunch and dinner every

---

12   Egusi soup - soup made of blended melon seeds and green leafy vegetables

13   Jollof-rice - Nigerian rice dish - usually orange in color. Cooked with blended tomatoes, red bell-peppers, onion, thyme, habanero pepper for spices, and many seasonings for taste.

day. I couldn't really complain. At least, they left something on their plates. When worst comes to worst, they might make me made *eba* to eat-which is made from *garri*. As always, Mom would visit and leave, working from the moment she got there until sundown. She would look at the scars on my body but not say a word. The only words she uttered were: "Remember the daughter of whom you are and never forget where you came from." She thanked them for their assistance in taking care of me and at the end of the day, they might give her some money for transportation back home. Then she would pick up her handbag and off she went, not knowing the next time I would see her.

CHAPTER SEVEN

JUST ANOTHER DAY

After Mom returned to Ilara, things continued as they were. The nights passed, and I continued to work. One and half years passed, and it was the same story. I stopped crying, but I continued to look unto God for hope. Hope was the only thing I had. Living with these people had not been easy. Every night, I talked to God and Dad. I was six and a half years old, soon to be seven, and I had never been to school. *God, I wish I could learn to read and write.* Every morning, I watched my mates go to school when I dropped off Kemi. I was acting like a slave while my mates were going to school. Washing, cleaning, cooking, and nurturing a child, I didn't have the time for other things. How could they expect a child to care for a toddler? Then, when I accidentally dropped the baby, which was many times, I got my life's beating: kneeling on the ground for several hours with my hands held up in the air, at some point I couldn't lift my hands, they were just so heavy. At that point, I would sob uncontrollably because of the pain.

After one and a half years, the family brought in another person. His name was Deji, and he was probably in his mid to late teens. Deji was tall and dark. Together, we did the house chores. But once again, similar to Wale, stealing was his hobby. This guy stole everything: money, food, even clothes. Unfortunately, I bore the brunt. If I told on him, he would beat me up when no one is home, but I would also get punished for the sins I did not commit if I said it was me. Either way, I got punished and beaten. The end of the story was that if I was not getting beat up by Mrs. Babalola's children, it was Deji. If it was not Deji, it was the witch herself.

Mr. and Mrs. Babalola had about seven children. Two females and five males. I heard of Yetunde, Steven, and Biola, but I had never seen them. So far, I had met Auntie Lola; who was the second daughter, and three of the boys—Ojo, Tayo, and Amos. Amos was the last born while Tayo was second to last. Once in a while, the three boys would come home, though not all at once. Through the years, I learned that Amos was Kemi's father. The story was: Amos got a young teen pregnant. After the girl was put to bed, she dropped Kemi at the doorstep and ran away. That was the end of the story. The girl never showed up. Mr. and Mrs. Babalola took full responsibility. After all, I think that was their first granddaughter, and they had no other choice but to keep her. I only wished Kemi would grow up one day to know the truth. They all pretended that Auntie Lola gave birth to her, but unfortunately, that was far from the truth. Although Amos was never made responsible and still lived a reckless life, he was nice. Actually, both Ojo and Amos were nice. They never scolded me; I hadn't met the rest of their boys.

The only devil beside Deji was Uncle Tayo. He was just like his mom, full of evil, and had so much hatred for me. Every time he came around, he tended to flog me with passion. One horrific Saturday afternoon, Mrs. Babalola and her husband had gone to one of their flamboyant parties. I will never forget this beating, and the worst part is I can't even remember what I was accused of or what I did. The only thing I can remember was saying, "I didn't do it." Tayo made me kneel on the ground for hours, holding my hands straight out to my sides, carrying heavy stones in both palms. Every time my hands shook, and the stone dropped, he whipped out his brown belt on his trousers and flogged me with it. He continued to do this until he got tired. I could tell his favorite part of the belt was the metal piece because he kept hitting me with it.

I prayed that someone should come to my rescue, but who? I knew that if the witch were here, she would probably take delight in my punishment, and I knew whatever I was being punished for, Deji had something to do with it. In the late evening, after being ordered to stand up from kneeling, I could barely walk. My legs trembled as I tried to stand up. With staggering gaits, I managed my way into the kitchen to boil water, dip a washcloth inside, and treat myself. I pressed the warm washcloth on my belt injuries. Deji came by the kitchen later, smiling and looking at me, and then walked away with a grin on his face. "Next time I tell you something, you better listen, and do as I said," he mumbled.

Mr. and Mrs. Babalola returned later at night. They didn't say much. Mrs. Babalola looked at me and then told me to get her bath water ready. She showered and went to bed. I finished performing my nightly chores and then put Kemi to bed. I hadn't cried myself to sleep for a while, but I couldn't help but cry on this day. I laid my night cloth on the ground, and all I could think of was the beating.

A few weeks later, I heard there was an altercation between Tayo and a random man while he was out with his friends. The man chewed off Tayo's middle finger and spat it out. Tayo was later rushed to the hospital to get the finger reattached. Mrs. Babalola rushed to the hospital to meet her son. Honestly, that was the best news ever. I was so happy on the inside. Never been so satisfied with a bad thing to happen to my enemy. For a moment, I was thankful to God for avenging me. When Tayo returned home, his finger was wrapped in a gauze bandage. It took a while for the finger to heal, and when it did, his finger never looked the same again, most especially his nail. Every time I walked past him, I couldn't help glancing at it with a smile.

About one and a half months later, Tayo was gone. I didn't see him in the house. I was surely happy about the scarcity of his face. His being around the house scared me, always worrying that he would beat me. He beat me with passion; that was his specialty.

A few months after Tayo left, another theft happened in the house. Mrs. Babalola should have known it was not me. Before Deji got there, nothing ever went missing. But ever since he showed up, things disappeared all the time. I had to lie that I did it because either way, it was a 'lose-lose' situation. That day was the worst. Mrs. Babalola went to grab a blade and made tiny cuts around my wrist. She then put dried powdered pepper and rubbed it on the wound. It was excruciating. My wrist felt like it was on fire. I cried until the pain was gone. "Next time it will be your other hand," she said.

After Tayo left, Ojo showed up. Uncle Ojo was the funny one and the ladies' man. Always picking up different ladies. A few times, I watched him bring new ladies to the house, take her to the room, and locked the door. I have also watched him run away from some ladies after being intimate with them. He urged me not to tell his whereabouts when a random lady came looking for him or tell them that he's not home. Any excuses to avoid seeing these ladies.

Uncle Ojo and Deji were close. They were so close that they shared rooms at times, the room located at the back of the house. As always, something went missing. Ojo summoned me up to his room, and asked me to kneel, raise my hands, and close my eyes. I did as he said. Then, he left. I didn't know how long he was gone, but he later returned with a belt. As he was about to hit me, he paused for a moment and then told me to get up and sit. I was so scared, and my body couldn't stop shivering.

"Come sit next to me," he said. Still shaken, I got up and sat on the ground near his foot. "Why do you keep stealing?" He asked.

I didn't say a word. I kept quiet. I looked for a moment, not realizing my eyes will gaze into his. Then I quickly looked away. I wanted to answer but just didn't bother. "I am sorry," I said. He lightly tapped me on my back and then urged me to go.

After three months, Deji was kicked out of the house. I didn't know what happened, but his mother came to beg Mr. and Mrs. Babalola. That was Deji's history of living with us and I couldn't be happier. Well, at least, things will not be disappearing in the house anymore. No more extra beating, no more being lied upon. This was a miracle. God, thank you for answering my prayer.

A month later, Mr. Babalola was in the living room when he summoned me. I ran as quickly as I can into the living room, dropping the task I was doing.

"Yes, sir," I said. I curtseyed to greet him. In Yoruba culture, female kneeling or curtseying was an appropriate way to greet elders or parents, while the male prostrates to the ground or bows their head.

"Can you raise or point to your right hand?" asked Mr. Babalola. I was confused. I pointed to my left. "Which one is your right hand?" he asked again. I stood there, looking dumbfounded and staring at the ground. I watched Mrs. Babalola come out of her room and sit on one of the couches. They both started insulting me. "Stupid girl! Dummy," they said.

"So, you do not know the difference between your right and left hand?" said Mr. Babalola. I continued staring at the ground. "You can leave," Mr. Babalola added.

"Thank you, sir… Ma", I said as I curtseyed, turned around, and ran back to the kitchen to finish cleaning up.

The following day, after taking Kemi to school, I went back to the house. God, I wish I could go to school to learn how to read and write. That would be very nice. I took out a piece of paper and began to make scribbles on the lines. I pretended I was writing in English and in full sentences. Talking to myself as I stood alone in the quiet room, pretending to be cleaning the clothes closet. For a moment, it was just me and the thoughts inside my head. Reading and writing, smiling and pretending that I had accomplished the world. I must admit that it was a great feeling until I heard footsteps, and reality set back in. I shoved the notebook into the clothes' piles in the closet and then began cleaning the room and making the beds.

Those days, I seemed to dream a lot. Lots of imagination, I must say. It served as my escape route, and whenever I was in my thoughts, I knew everything would be okay. Sometimes, I dreamt of living in this awesome place; it was a strange land. I was standing by the glass window in the dream, watching something white falling from the sky. Watching indoors, the white flakes brought about a sense of calmness; peace. I stood by the lonely window, watching God's beautiful creation. I could feel the cold and see the condensation of mixtures of my breath and the cold air on the glass window. When I woke up in the morning, sometimes, I wondered what this dream meant.

Other times, I imagined talking to my dad in my dreams. Even though his face seemed to fade per dream, I could barely remember what he looked like. Yet, I still tried holding on to the memory of him being alive. My only vivid recollection of him was when we were sitting in the taxicab and trying to get his attention and he wearing that dark sunshade. That was the only time we ever sat together actually. Dad was never around. So, I never got to know or see him.

One beautiful night, I was asked to go buy *akara*[14], a loaf of bread, and Guinness beer. It was around 9 P.M. The stars were out and looked so mesmerizing that I couldn't help but stare. A gentle breeze kissed my face. I closed my eyes and made a wish, hoping my dream would come true. I saw all kinds of people living largely among each other with no suffering in my dream. At times, they all wear hats and huge clothes and shoes that went to their knees. When they spoke, their words and dictions were fascinating. I wished I were there to dine and wine with them; a place where all my sorrows could disappear. I closed my eyes and made this wish; a wish for a better life and to live in a better place. When I opened my eyes, I felt a great sense of relief. I feel revived with a rush of positive energy. I started smiling like I had just won a lottery ticket. Then, I started running to the joint before it closes. The last thing I wanted that night was to get punished and for my mood to get destroyed. I hurried along and returned to the house. When everyone was sleeping, I stargazed into the sky, smiling while finishing my chores. The night looked peaceful.

From that moment, each night, I imagined myself in a different world: a world where I was not suffering or begging before I could eat; a world where I had so many opportunities to better myself and to rid myself of this

---

14   Akara - fried beans cake

poverty I was born into; a world where I could make my mom proud.

That was how it was for a long time. For every tough moment, I cleaved to that breezy peaceful night. A night like that hardly comes and on a night like that, I knew everything would be okay.

CHAPTER EIGHT

A NEW BEGINNING; A NEW ME

Six months before I turned eight, Mr. Babalola summoned me into the living room. "Starting Tuesday, you will be starting school," he said. I guess after discovering that I didn't know my left hand from my right or my birthday or age, he figured he should enroll me in school. I remember the sound of his voice on that very day: disappointment and shame. He must have been ashamed of me. To keep a child and for that child not to know anything is disgraceful. But seriously, you can't blame me. I had never celebrated my birthday or been to school. Shocked and not knowing what to do or say, I stood still in the living room, waiting for what would happen next. I then got down on my knees, bowed my head, and thanked him for his gracious generosity. I glanced at him, but I noted he didn't smile or reply to my gratitude.

He ordered me to get up, but before I could stand, Mrs. Babalola came out of the bedroom and sat on one of the sofas. "This doesn't change anything. You'll go to school and come back to do all the house chores," she said in her usual hostile voice. The only time she was not angrily yelling was when she was on the phone talking to her high-class group of friends. Even then, she was very obnoxious, always snapping her gum while talking at the top of her voice like she is the only person in the house. Mrs. Babalola was always chewing on bubble gum. She had packs of them in her bedroom, and the worst part: when she was done, she would take them out of her mouth and stick them to any surface she could find; either be her bed linens, sofas, tables, walls, cups, plates, the list goes on. Mrs. Babalola loved to take control and dominate everything. Whatever she said, that was what would happen. I had never seen anyone stand against her, not even her husband. All Mr. Babalola did was stay silent. He never had the guts to stand up for anything. He was calm and quiet in his demeanor. Mrs. Babalola was the opposite: short tempered and hostile.

The only thing this witch did was order people around. She spent so much money living extravagantly, wearing all kinds of lace materials, new handbags, and shoes. She paraded herself everywhere like she owned the entire town. The fact that the family didn't work was another thing. She and her husband had never worked a day since I had been living with them. All they did was wake up and eat. *So, how do they get the money?* Although I heard they were a royal family, they were not heir to the throne or any such thing. They were just a lineage of royalty. And being a lineage doesn't generate any sort of income, most especially in Nigeria. I was certain that the small apartment complex rented to their tenants was not enough to run a whole town. So, where was the money coming from?

It was surprising that every time people came to the house, they went on their knees to beg. Mrs. Babalola loved being in power. She treated everyone who was not the same social status as her like peasants, including children and widows. She and her group of friends were the real demons. I could swear they belonged to a cult group. Her cult must have been sacrificing humans for their wealth. Two of her friends had come to the house on different occasions. Their excessive make-up made them look pasty and yellow like a witch. I didn't understand how someone could be so evil and vindictive. Every time they came into the house, all they did was stare me down.

Mrs. Akin was worse than Mrs. Babalola if I must say. She was always sending me on errands and telling me to hurry up. "Run, and don't let me see those puny legs of yours on the ground," she would say and then turn her head and laugh with Mrs. Babalola. As a visitor, I didn't think she had the right to send me up and down. But in this house, this was how things worked. If either of them called and I didn't run to meet them immediately, it was a slap on my face. It seemed they both loved the injustice they were inflicting on me.

Nigerians believe in witches, and not the ones with green faces and flying brooms. Nigerian witches were usually referred to as humans; people who live as humans during the day and as spirits at night. At night, their soul quit their bodies and assume the form of a creature or themselves; only their leaders could operate during the day. Others use babalawo[15,] a herbalist or native diviner. They use their power to communicate with IFA[16] to determine their client's future. Although many classify this as evil. Before the introduction of Christianity to Africa, these were the ways of life and how Africa practiced their faith. In today's world, the practice of IFA is considered evil by many. By Babalawo chanting incarnation, they are able to communicate with their gods and grant and accomplish the evil deeds for their clients. Using Voodoos[17] and herbalists, they summoned people's souls; souls that are not strong in Christ, and they attacked them, spiritually. They may even attack the young and use them for money rituals to gain power and wealth.

For this reason, many churches were built. On every street corner, there are up to five churches. When you are in Nigeria, you learn that just because someone attends church doesn't mean their heart is pure. Too many fake prophets everywhere. Sunday after Sunday, people are in church praying and casting out demons and witches. They also spend time doing evangelism to win souls.

So, I believed this woman was doing something shady. She and her friends must be sacrificing humans to obtain money and power. This is called the ultimate hu-

---

15   Babalawo - herbalist- faith diviner, ones who communicate with IFA for spiritual consultations.

16   IFA-- Indigenous Faith of Africa (divination system that teaches the teaching of Orisha; Yoruba religion practices)

17   Voodoo(s) - black religious cult; a molded idol that is believed to possess spiritual powers/characterized by sorcery.

man ritual[18]. This belief is widespread in Nigeria. People will do anything to obtain money and be in power. In my country, money speaks. By having money, people in high power can get away with murder. All you have to do is bribe the lawmakers, judges, and or the police. They would allow the perpetrator to go scot-free while the innocent will be convicted. The only problem was that she and her friends could not touch me. I bore the mark of God. I was born in the house of God for a reason. I prayed each day that "no weapons fashioned against me shall prosper," according to the Bible. My stronghold of God gave me the courage, and deep down, I knew nothing she did could harm me. So, the only thing she could do was maltreat me.

I continued to kneel while Mr. Babalola added, "Tuesday, you'll be starting Saint Joseph Primary School."

"Thank you, sir," I said to show my appreciation. This is my new beginning. Thank you, Jesus! God has answered my prayers. Finally! I got a chance to step out of this house. I continued to kneel until they ordered me to get up.

"You can go now," he said. I thanked them both once more and then ran to the kitchen to continue preparing dinner.

"And hurry up! We are starving," Mrs. Babalola shouted.

---

18   Human rituals - the practice of killing humans and harvesting body parts (head, organs, kidney, hearts, etc…) and offering it to the gods/ herbalists to generate wealth and power.

After dinner, Mrs. Babalola gave me ten naira to use to get my hair shaved. "Go and get your hair cut tomorrow." Then, she threw a uniform with a pair of brown sandals at me. The plaid red and white uniform hit my face and fell on the red carpet. I picked it up.

"Thank you, ma." I waited a while until Mr. Babalola asked me to leave.

The next day, I woke up early, got the house ready, made breakfast, and got Kemi prepared for school. By 7 A.M., breakfast was available and placed on the dining table. I made boiled yams and fried eggs, and boiled water, and served them in a flask to keep them hot, and then I placed Lipton tea bags on the side of their tray. The Babalola family loved tea. It was a must have. Without tea, their breakfast was not complete. I fed Kemi, made Indomies[19] for her lunch, and off I went to drop her at school. On our way, I could not stop thinking about how exciting it would be to finally go to school.

Returning home, I went straight to the barbershop to get my hair shaved. In almost all Nigerian public schools, both male and female students have to get their hair cut unless they attend private schools. Everything is about discipline. Nigerian values the importance of teaching kids discipline and respect. Hair and nails must be cut and kept clean at all times. Uniforms must be cleaned and pressed with an iron, with no mess and no stain. Every child wears a uniform as long as they are in school. This is how the school system works until students are in senior secondary or tertiary schools. At that time, the female students can do whatever they want, which gives

---

19   Indomies - instant noodles

them the freedom to braid their hair and dress modestly, which is presentable to society's eyes. Back then, they believed that females plaiting their hair in the early stage prevented learning and distracts both genders. Children dressing alike in their primary and secondary school years prevent sexual attention among the students and promote educational competitions. Education competitions promote better I.Q.s. That's why you will find most Nigerian parents wanting their children to be lawyers, doctors, or engineers. It's like those are the only jobs in the world. Part of the demands for these occupations is because they want to show off their children to their peers. Moreover, they know that any of the three occupations will generate significant income, placing the family into a well standard high class. Nigerian values prestige, title, and educational background. That's why you'll find a Ph.D. holder in some of the households of people who can afford education. Abroad, Nigerians are known to be brilliant, dedicated, and educated. We dedicated our lives to being schooled, studying to become someone great in order to help our family. So, in the end, we can be referred by our title; doctor, missus; barrister, bishop, all just to be signify that they are well read or some sort. Some will list all the titles before their name. To be marry in Nigeria is potent most especially for women. A successful woman who is unmarried is subject to mockery by society. It seems as if all her accomplishments are nothing without a man by her side. As Nigerians would say, you need a man to be your head. You need a man to lead. That is why it is not just Dr. Adegero, but doctor missus as my mom always referred to her. The missus is to signify to everyone that she is married.

Tuesday morning felt like a million years away. I was asleep by midnight, and by four-thirty in the morning, I was up, did my morning chores, got Kemi ready, prepared breakfast, and served it. By 6:50 A.M., I was done and out of the house. Saint Joseph started at 8:00 A.M., and I could not afford to be late on my first day. The last thing I wanted was to get disciplined at school for being late. The school gate closed at 8 A.M. After dropping Kemi, I ran miles to get to school. In my hand were my pencil and one blue notebook, all inside a plastic bag. I didn't have much for school supplies. If you were poor like me, plastic bags are your backpack. By the time I arrived, I was drenched in sweat. I was exhausted.

The first day of school was exciting. Third grade was not easy. In Math class, we wrote our multiplication tables several times on lined paper. We also recite it multiple times. English class was very challenging because learning the English language was something new to me. I couldn't even pronounce most of the words on the blackboard. After long hours of class, we had a recess. I hated recess time. Recess was packed with many older and younger students than I. Some students went outside the gates to buy food, while others stayed inside the school premises. There were too many people outside. I hated break time. Most times, I sat in one corner and watch people eat their lunch. I didn't have money to be buying food, so all I could do is go back into the classroom and wait until the class returned to session.

After the lunch break, we headed to another classroom. This was where we spent our afternoon until the school closed. We spent all morning in one classroom and afternoon in another. School ended at 2:30 P.M. School ending was the worst thing that could ever happen. As the time approached, my mind started to wander, my heart beating so fast as if I was going to faint. Once school ended, I headed straight home. On my way, I stopped to pick up Kemi from her school. Kemi's school was only a block from the house.

Months passed and it was the same old routine. I could now balance the house chores and school. The school was not bad but could have been better. The best part about going to school was that it gave me the chance to step out of the house; the worst part was English class. I sucked in the English language. I couldn't read. Sometimes, our teacher walked around, asking some of the students to read what was written on the chalkboard. Each time she did that, my heart pounded, hoping that I wouldn't get called. I kept thinking about how stupid I felt when Mr. Babalola asked me to differentiate between my left and right hands. I was always afraid of making mistakes or saying the wrong thing. The discipline and beating had gotten me shaken up so that I avoided mistakes. On the other side, math was my favorite subject. I loved numbers, and I could do calculations all day.

The other worst part of school was not making friends. I found it extremely difficult to relate to others. I was not the type of person to have many friends. But after a while, I finally made a friend named Yemi. She was cool. Sometimes, we walked home together, but she had to walk farther. I was not sure if I could consider her a true friend, but I'd watch and see for now. I was very selective of people I called friends.

After a while, I became my teachers' favorite. I was that good in school, and oh yes, I liked that. I think that was God's favor. Sometimes, students bought me food and snacks. Other times, the teacher would buy me lunch but not all the time. They couldn't show favoritism in front of others. Despite the supportive school friends and those we walked home together; I wasn't happy. I was always quiet and hanging by myself. One day, one of the older female students and her group of friends came around me, teasing me. They were the bullies of the school. They picked on most students, taking their lunches, and calling them all sorts of names. Most people were afraid of them. Students always ran into hiding when they approached. That day, I was sitting alone outside during lunch break when the group approached me. Making fun of me and calling me the school geek, their words didn't hold water. So, I didn't react. Then, the leader of the group pulled my shirt, saying that I stink. I was bitterly angry and didn't know what happened. The next thing I knew was that I was punching the girl in her face. I was not going to let anyone bully me. Not for my dress or for being poor. I was poor. And yes, but I didn't need anyone to make me feel worse than I already feel at home

Growing up in Nigeria teaches you to be headstrong. If you don't defend yourself among your peers, then you'll be their pounding flesh. It is a dog-eat-dog world. A typical Nigerian parent will smack you for coming home to cry instead of defending yourself. They do not raise a spineless child, some will say.

I didn't know what happened to me, but I was fighting students all the time, including older students. I guess I was frustrated with the world. Ever since the day I fought the ringleader, the group never bothered me again. Honestly, they never disturbed any students again. The group leader burst into tears, and we both got in trouble with the teacher for fighting. Since then, I became a fighter for students, most especially for students who were considered weaklings.

On many occasions, I got in trouble with teachers for fighting, but they grew tired after a while. The news traveled back home, and the Babalolas heard everything. Surprisingly, the family never said anything. After a while, we took the fight outside the school premises. It was not as if I liked fighting. I just despised people maltreating the innocent. I might not be able to speak up at home, but the school would be different. I would fight anyone who thought they could say anything negative about me. I would not tolerate it.

Apart from school, which provided me with a place where I forgot my worries, the home remained miserable. Same thing, every day. In school, nobody knew my struggles except our surrounding neighbors and tenants. But who were they to meddle with someone else's business? Everyone minded their businesses and families. A husband could be beating his wife to death, and no one would intervene. This is how some societies in Nigeria operate. Everyone is afraid to get involved in a couple's misunderstanding, but they can gossip like no other. Their gossip and busybody attitudes can make one scurry into a hole. So much hatred for one another, but at the same time, they called themselves Christians. From what I know, being Christ-like is being humble: treating everyone with kindness and not the other way around.

Many months later, Amos and Tayo came home. At first, I was upset that this Tayo of a thing was back. Luckily, they didn't stay too long, and one month after, Kemi was gone. Where he took her, I don't know. Now I was the only child in the house. Kemi being gone reduced my workload. I continued to go to school and come home to be a maid. This new life wasn't bad. I didn't get beaten as I was used to. The best part was going to school. I was finally learning to read and write but mostly in Yoruba. To speak in Yoruba is different from reading and writing it. To speak a language is something everyone knows how to do, but to be able to read and write in that language is another. Not most people who know how to speak can write. I wanted a better life for myself.

I laid in bed most nights, wondering what changed Mr. and Mrs. Babalola. Why did they decide to enroll me in school? Many people and children had lived with them in the past, but none of them had ever been sent to school. What changed? Don't get me wrong. Mrs. Babalola was still wicked. Countless times, she reminded me of my poor background and my helpless widowed mother. I still woke up at the same time each day to prep meals and clean the house. I still had to fetch water from the well and refill all the emptied containers. I still had to hand wash all their clothes, including their undergarments, and spread them to dry. Most of all, I hated weekends because I worked all day and night, from one task to another. I knew I didn't have a normal life, which was the main reason I didn't surround myself with friends from school. Everyone was on their own, facing their battles and the daily challenges of life.

Similarly, most children that come from poor families don't have time for friends. That people like us had the opportunity to go to school was by God's grace. After school, we usually ran back home to help our mothers in the market, selling produce on the street to help feed the family. No sales mean no money for food. It's a cycle. Without income, you couldn't do or afford anything. Eventually, we would have to drop out of school, which placed us back in the endless circle of poverty and surviving to live. This is life in Nigeria with a lack of good leaders and government to alleviate the lower- and middle-class families. So, for this reason, I thanked the Babalolas every day because I was just fortunate enough to go to school. Maybe someday, I would make a difference, break the cycle of poverty, and change my family life. I was fortunate that I didn't have to hawk goods on my head, selling them from street to street. I had been there, and that chapter of my life was closed.

Despite everything, I never complained. I continued to be myself. I respected the Babalolas, but it was out of fear. I never abused my freedom of being allowed to go to school. I went to school and returned home immediately. I thanked them every blessed day, for sending me to school. Mrs. Babalola love being praised. A little kindness was like you owed them your life.

CHAPTER NINE

NEW WORLD

Although I was scolded less, I was still very bitter. I was exhausted but at the same time, fearful. I was afraid for my life and my mom's. For some reason, Mom never visited again. The worst part: I didn't even remember what my sisters looked like. After a while, it felt like I didn't have a family or siblings. It was just me, alone. I felt so lost in this world. The last time I got a visit from home was when Esther, my second eldest sister visited. We cooked that day and everyone ate. Uncle Ojo gave me the rest of his food. I decided to share it with Esther and when Mrs. Babalola saw us eating outside in the yard, she started shouting like a raging dog and creating a scene. She asked who gave us the food or if we stole it. Before I could say it was Uncle Ojo, she insulted us and walked away. When she later found out the truth from Uncle Ojo, she hissed. Esther and I got into argument that day. She said I should never offer her food or anything again. And immediately she left and went back to Ilara. That was the end of sister Esther. I never saw her again. So, since then, I haven't seen any family members.

Not Mom or my sisters. No matter what, I always prayed. I prayed to God to heal my heart.

After all the fights from school, Mr. and Mrs. Babalola called me into the living room one of the days. They informed me that it would be beneficial if I start attending church. After many years of living with this couple, who would have thought they would finally allow me to go to church. First, it was school, and now, it was the church. "There is a church behind the house," Mr. Babalola said. Behind the house was a small local broken-down wooden church. I had walked past the place every day when I dropped off Kemi at her school. Based on its looks, people could hardly tell it was a place of worship. Inside the church, there was hardly any chairs. It was just a log of wood serving as chairs. But every Sunday, the six to eight of us gathered to sing, pray, and worship. We did our short church service and headed home.

The church people were friendly. I went to church every Sunday, but still, I wasn't happy. My heart was hurting, and no amount of praying seemed to help. Maybe, they knew I was hurting, and for this reason, they allowed me to start attending church, or perhaps it was because they were starting to develop human feelings towards me. For this family to treat me as a human rather than a fatherless village girl seemed impossible. I heard a saying that when you live with a person for a long time, they will start taking an interest in the individual. Maybe, this was the case. But I doubt that.

From what I've heard, nobody had ever lived with them for that long. I had been living with them for years, and she still maltreated me every chance she got. Mrs.

Babalola, in particular, hated me with a passion. But for odd reasons, she allowed her husband to send me to school and church. Again, when I think about it, maybe I was wrong about her husband, maybe he did have some type of influence over his wife. Mr. Babalola was a nice man. He was quiet and somewhat gentle. The only problem was he never said a word. He mostly watched and allowed his wife to maltreat people and take control of everything.

Maybe Mrs. Babalola would start to know me for who I am? They could not deny that I was a good child. I was indeed a great child. Every time they called me, I dropped everything and ran like a lightning bolt to meet their demands. I was a hard worker. So, I think they liked me for that. I could work from morning to night without food in my system, without getting tired. Concerning food, I didn't even bother to eat until they offered me meals or their remains on their plates. I did and faced all this without complaint. The best part: they thought I stopped stealing. Ever since Deji had left, nothing went missing anymore. I never allowed my school attitudes and behaviors to impact my work at home. To top it off, I was smart, and brilliant in math.

One random Saturday, Mr. Babalola sent me to get my photo taken by the photo shop in front of the house. I put on my blue native attire, a skirt and blouse. I didn't know what it was for, but my job was to do as I was told and never to question them. A few days later, the photo was ready: it was tiny. And man! It looked like a toy. So, this was a two-by-two size photo. I got home and gave it to Mr. Babalola. Afterwards, that was it. I never heard anything about the photo. I continued to go to school, and take care of the house, and the Babalolas. These days, there were fewer complaints, but Mrs. Babalola had her moments, most especially when she was in a bad mood. At times, she would insult me and call my mom a beggar. "Look at the person that we are trying to help?" she would say while walking away.

This was how it was for a long time until one day. Mrs. Babalola told me to start growing my hair, so I did. I was confused, but never did I ask questions like, "What about school?" I could get into trouble with the school-teachers for not shaving my hair or maintaining a low cut. She also handed me a brand-new pair of red trousers, a white shirt with a pink design on the front of it, and a black covered flat shoe. The pants looked cute, but I had never worn trousers in my life. My family's faith forbade us from wearing pants. Being a CAC believer, wearing pieces of jewelry and trousers was considered a sin. My family always wore skirts; skirts that were below the knees or at the ankles. We never wore any shirts that exposed our back, chest, or shoulders. Nigeria is a conservative nation. Any woman or young adult exposing her body will be deemed a prostitute. The societies viewed these as sins because they considered the person impure. Also, we believe that the things meant for the future husband should be kept hidden from the world. I grew up in a family and society where Mom and Dad had never allowed us to wear such things. Trousers are considered men's wear. And things that belong to men should never be worn by women and vice versa.

When I told her that I could not wear the pants, she burst into laughter and shouted, "Get in the room and try on the clothes! You, this ungrateful child. Instead of you saying thank you, you are saying nonsense…. I can't wear these pants," she mumbled. I dashed inside and tried on the new pair of pants. It fitted. She knew my size! *Woah, these pants are adorable. Why is she buying me new things? Am I going somewhere? This is interesting.*

That was that until two months after the New Year. In the late morning, we got into Mr. Babalola's green vehicle and we traveled to a place I have never been there before. There were police officers and security guards everywhere. Along the way, I couldn't help but stare outside the window. It looked nice, but not long after, I started to feel sick to my stomach. My stomach began to rumble, and I couldn't help feeling I might vomit soon. I held my stomach and closed my eyes until we arrived at our destination. It was a long journey. We got out of the car and headed straight to the information desk. Behind the office was a man in a black suit. I had never seen such skin color before. His skin tone was pale. Silky and smooth hair texture. This man looked different from the people I saw daily.

Moments later, the man looked down at him, then turned back and continued to ask Mr. and Mrs. Babalola questions. "You are her parents? Are you sure?" The white man said.

"Yes, she's our child," replied Mrs. Babalola. Then Mr. Babalola signaled to his wife. I watched her reach into her purse, took out some documents, and then handed them over to the man behind the desk. The man took the papers, looked at them, stamped them, and then handed them back. I supposed he asked them all those questions because they were old. Too old to give birth to someone as young as me.

After the long wait of back-and-forth questioning and answers, we were done. We headed back into the car. For the rest of the week, we stayed with their friends, who lived around the area. I only wished I knew where we were. This place didn't look anywhere near Akure. Here, the atmosphere looked better with better roads, buildings, and somewhat stable electricity. Maybe, they were using generators. Nigeria never has stable electricity. Mr. and Mrs. Babalola's friend's house was amazing with a nice flat-screen television, the biggest that I had ever seen. The TV we had at the house was boxy and bulky. Kemi always watched Barney on it. But this TV was impressive. The picture quality was crystal clear. The people on the screen looked like that man in the embassy, they had the same skin and hair texture. Actually, that was the very first time that the Babalolas were allowing me to watch TV. I lay there on the ground, watching the soap opera, even though I did not understand what they were saying.

As the week came to an end, we headed back to Akure. It was like nothing happened. I wished I had someone to talk to about this. I had no friends, neither did I keep any. Somebody had to know where we went. Maybe, it was Lagos or Abuja. I just had to keep it off my mind and focus on reality. Were they trying to sell me to another person? For days, these questions ricocheted in my mind. I had to tell someone, maybe Yemi. Over the years, we had become close friends. Well, just school friends anyway. Yemi was tall and dark. Actually, everyone I knew was taller than me. I am short and don't look my age. The only thing I have are these cheeks. Man! I have chubby cheeks.

Monday approached, and I told Yemi all about my adventures. The next day, she came back and told me I went to Lagos. "How do you know?" I asked.

"Oh… I asked my sisters. They said it's probably US Embassy in Lagos. Listen, my sisters think your family is traveling to ilu-oyinbo[20]," she said.

Ilu-oyinbo means white men's land. I was as confused as before. "I told you not to tell anybody," I said to her, but she didn't say anything. Then, she stated, "I thought you wanted to know where your family takes you?" Yemi didn't know the Babalolas were not my biological family, but rather, a strange family who proclaim to have known my father when he was alive. They claim my father was an amazing man of God and he had helped them on many occasions. I know Dad would be turning in his grave if he knew this is how they treated his family.

Anyway, I looked at Yemi, walked away and didn't answer. This just proved that she couldn't be trusted. Before the end of the week, some people in school had already found out. How was this possible? Man, people have a big mouth.

On Friday evening, while cooking, as always, the family summoned me up to the living room. They asked me

---

20   Ilu-oyinbo - white man's land/abroad. Ilu - means country; oyinbo - means white man's

who have you been telling and talking to? I kept still and quiet.

"Go back. When you get back to school on Monday, make sure you tell people you are not traveling anywhere. Do you understand what is coming out of my mouth?" Mrs. Babalola said.

"Yes, ma," I replied.

"Who wants to take you anywhere, just look at you? Have you seen yourself in the mirror? Get out!" She shouted.

I hurried along and back into the kitchen. Yemi had gotten me into trouble. People could not be trusted. By the following Monday, everyone in the class already knew about my trip. Everyone kept asking when I am leaving for the States. At lunchtime, everyone gathered around to hear about my plan to travel outside the country. Sadly, I had to break the news.

"I am not traveling anywhere. This is all rumors." I said. "I don't know where the rumors started, but it's not true."

Everyone looked at each other then, they dispersed. Boy, I was glad that was all over. Now, I know not to tell anyone anything anymore. Besides, I never said I was traveling to the States. Those words never came out of my mouth. Months passed, and things at school went back to normal. Nobody bothered to ask me any questions anymore.

On an early Friday morning in May, the family left the house and headed to Lagos. I got up, cleaned the house, and before sunrise, we were dressed and out the door. I was wearing my red trousers and the white shirt they bought me. They never told anyone about the trip. The thing with Nigeria is they always believe in a conspiracy that someone is out to get them. If any mishap happens, it's the devil or the village people, or it's the ancestors that are after their success. We finished packing the luggage and place them inside the car trunk—so much luggage.

I wondered where we were going. I sat in the back of the car, Mrs. Babalola next to me, and Mr. Babalola seated on the passenger seat. After many hours on the road, I finally saw the logo banner: "This is Lagos!" It was boldly inscribed on a big screen. Wow! Yemi's sisters were right. But how come I never noticed this sign the first day we traveled? We passed the sign and continued to drive onward. Then, we got to the sign that read, "Murtala Muhammed International Airport." Looking at the big sign, my heart dropped to my chest. *Where are these people taking me? What about my mom and my sisters? I have not seen them in years. This family has never treated me like a human being so, where are we possibly heading? Are they selling me?* We arrived at the airport, and the driver helped us carry the pieces of luggage inside. He then spoke with Mr. Babalola and drove the car away.

CHAPTER TEN

BROCKTON, MASSACHUSETTS

We entered the airport and proceeded to the information desk and then got in the line to check in the luggage. There was a lady behind the desk. Mr. Babalola weighed each piece of luggage, and I noticed a tag was placed on them, one after the other. At times, we had to move things around and then reweigh the bags. After checking in our luggage, we went through a security screening. I watched people remove their shoes, belts, purses, backpacks, and so on, and I did the same. I took off my shoes and went through the metal detectors. Standing at the opposite sides were ladies and gentlemen, one at each end, patting people down from head to toes. They patted us down too, and then they allowed us to put on our gear at the other end. We grabbed our carry-ons and headed straight to our boarding gate. When it was time, the flight crew called us, and we boarded the airplane. Walking through the tunnel led us to two travel agents at the end. They checked our tickets and then directed us to our row. I walked behind Mrs. Babalola through the aisle. Finally, we found our seats.

I watched Mr. Babalola place our carry-ons overhead and close the storage compartment. The plane was filled with so many people as I glanced around. Mrs. Babalola ordered me to have a seat in the middle. I grabbed my seat and sat down quietly. I stared at the pamphlet in the seat pocket; trying not to make eye contact with anyone.

Thirty minutes passed, and the flight attendants urged everyone to take their seats. "Welcome to Delta Airline," a voice came on over the intercom. "At this time, I would like everyone to fasten their seatbelt," the female voice said. After the greeting, two flight attendants stood in each aisle to demonstrate how to use the emergency equipment. Also, there was guided imagery being displayed on the mini television screen, depicting what to do in case of an emergency. I picked up the pamphlet located in the pocket on the back of the seat. Mrs. Babalola looked at me but didn't say a word; she instead gave me stinky eyes. I returned the pamphlet to the pocket and looked at the screen.

Being on a plane for the very first time was the scariest thing ever. After taking off from the ground, the plane wouldn't stop shaking. It was a rough flight. My ears could not help but feel full. It felt like they were going to pop. At times, the plane shook terribly, and I'd closed my eyes, holding on to the seat firmly and praying that God landed us safely. The family never said anything. Multiple times, they got up to use the restroom. I just sat there in the middle, not uttering a word.

Many hours passed, and we were still on the flight. Falling asleep and waking up with meals being served in-between. The moment we landed, many people rushed out of the plane, dragging their carry-on behind them. I was sure glad the flight was over. Well, I thought it was until I realized that we had another plane to board. We walked out of the tunnel and joined the crowd of people at the airport. Using the moving escalators was also scary, but once I got used to it, it was easy. I loved it, and if I had the chance, I would ride it all day. Mr. Babalola led the way. Finding our connecting flight was the most stressful, but the beautiful scenery took away the pain that came with it. The stores were beautiful with bright colors. I wished we could go inside, but that was not going to happen. The airport itself was amazing but cold. The lights were crystal clear, twinkling, and bright. This place was quite different from home.

I didn't know that many people traveled like this. It must be amazing to travel and visit different countries. If only I had money. I decided when I grow up, I would like to travel to different countries. Anyways, boarding the second flight was the same process as the first. If I thought the first flight was long, the connecting flight seemed longer. This time, I sat near the window. I never thought I would like the window seat. I didn't have to keep getting up for them to use the restroom. A few times, I woke up and peeked to see if the Babalolas were awake, and when I realized they were sleeping, I opened the window shade and looked into the sky. At one point, it was the middle of the night. The sky was pitch black. Staring into the sky was breathtaking. The airplane wing was amazing and long. Before I knew it, I was back to sleep once again. Hours later, when I woke up, this time more people were awake. The flight attendants offered snacks and drinks. Not knowing what to do, I shook my head and rejected their offers. Mrs. Babalola looked at me and I looked down.

I sat there long enough without motions. At times, I needed to use the bathroom but was scared to speak up. I just held on to my urine. After a while, I couldn't take it anymore. I looked at Mrs. Babalola, and she knew that I needed to use the restroom. She got up and walked me to the bathroom and waited for me to finish. It was the smallest bathroom that I had ever been in. When I finished, we headed back to our seats. Ten hours of flight, and we finally landed. One hour prior, handouts were given. Mr. Babalola collected it and filled out the forms. One for him, me, and the wife.

"Ladies and gentlemen, welcome to Boston. The time now is 3:45 P.M. The forecast in Boston is 68 degrees Fahrenheit and it is cloudy with a chance of rain. Please enjoy your stay," announced over the intercom. The pilot parked the plane, and everyone began getting off their seats, grabbing their small luggage from the cabin.

Is this it? Is the flight over? I could not believe my eyes. Flying on the plane felt like an eternity. I was sure glad it was over. The ride was so emotional. At times, I cried, thinking about home, my mom, and my siblings, but at the same time, I could not help but wonder if they cared about me. Mom had given me away, and returning home didn't seem like an option. This family had completely changed my identity. Staring at the green colored Nigerian passport in Mr. Babalola's hand, I figured it was mine because it had the snapshot of my photo. It was the same photo they once sent me to get taken near the house. Staring at it, I realized I no longer bore my father's last name but instead Babalola. My father's name has been changed to my middle name. When it came to giving names to children in Nigeria, the child tends to have multiple names from each grandparent and in-laws. I bear many names, but now, it was just three: first, middle, and surname in my new documents. It seemed like the other names no longer existed. My identity might be gone, but I will always know who I am and the daughter of whom I belong.

More security checks after getting off the plane. We went through customs, then proceed to sign that read, "baggage claims." At the baggage claims, we couldn't find all our bags. We then ended at another place where there were many other traveling suitcases. Standing there were security dogs and officers in uniform. They made us open our luggage and after checking what was inside, they let us go. I wonder what the deal with that was. I guess they figured it was just food and nothing else. Maybe, we were not supposed to bring food across the country. Anyway, we picked up our bags and luggage, then headed outside to the pickup station. Boston sure was busy and beautiful. The roads, the lights, and the people. The people all looked different. They are all so different from me. I like this. It's unique and mind-blowing. I wished I could speak just like them. We headed outside, dragging luggage one after the other.

By the pickup station was Uncle Amos, standing next to a dark green car. Uncle Amos bent his head and greeted his parents. "How are you, and how's everyone?" Mr. Babalola asked.

"They are good, sir," he replied. He helped us load the suitcases into the car trunk, and I helped him. We then got into the car, and Uncle Amos started driving. It was a long ride home. Along the way, I couldn't help but sleep. Several times, I woke up to look outside the window only to fall back asleep. Although it started to drizzle, I couldn't help being mesmerized by this beautiful country. I had never seen any road or street that was that was well built. The trees were green, and the houses were well constructed. Amazing! The atmosphere was clean, and every breath of air was fresh.

Akure, on the other hand, was the complete opposite. The roads were horrific, with many potholes and unpaved ground. Every wind that blows brings about dusty red sand, causing it to stain your clothes as you walk. This is one of the reasons clothes don't last long before they fade. The environment is hot and has too much polluted air.

I peeked at Mrs. Babalola. She was wide awake. *Oh boy, this woman scares me,* I thought. I turned my head quickly, looked outside, and closed my eyes. I didn't know when I fell back to sleep, but the next time I woke up, we were at the exit to Brockton. I shut my eyes and pretended to be asleep. Not long after, the car stopped. We arrived at a white house with a red colored door. Mrs. Babalola opened the door and tapped me to get up. I got out of the car and watched as she and her husband went inside. Uncle Amos and I stayed outside to carry the luggage inside.

Woah! This house is big. Nice house. As I came in, a woman came downstairs, shouting in a joyful voice. "Yetunde! Omo mi, bawo ni[21]?" Mrs. Babalola said. The lady hugged her mother and slightly bent her knees to greet her dad, followed by a hug.

"Grandma! Grandpa!" two little girls came out, hugging them.

"Renee! Ashley!" replied both Mr. and Mrs. Babalola. "My little angels," Mrs. Babalola said.

Moments later, Kemi came down. She ran to hug them. She seemed so happy. So, this was where Kemi had been the whole time she was gone. She was a big girl now. Wow… This house is full. As a matter of fact, full was an understatement. There in the house was Auntie Yetunde, her four children—two girls and two boys: Renee, Ashley, Demola, who was a year old, and Raphael, who was only a few months. Also, there was Kemi, Mr. and Mrs. Babalola, Amos, and an older grandma, whom the kids called Mama. She must be the other mother-in-law. I wondered where Auntie Yetunde's husband was.

I stood there while everyone exchanged greetings. Auntie Yetunde approached me, and I curtseyed to greet her. She touched my shoulder as she asked me how I was doing in Yoruba. So, this was the almighty Yetunde, the one Mrs. Babalola always talked with on the phone. I prayed she was nice, just like Auntie Lola, her younger sister. I hoped she liked me. *God, please let her like me*, I prayed.

---

21   Omo mi, bawo ni - my child, how are you?

The girls looked at me but didn't utter a word, instead they smiled and ran to the living room to play. They were cute but looked extremely spoilt. I stared at them, and I wished I had their lives. They didn't even know what it felt like to go through struggles or to not have a family. They probably got everything they wanted. I guess this was the reason why Mrs. Babalola brought me, to be their maid. But that doesn't explain why they changed my identity. With all these people living here, I was sure they'd need assistance.

The evening was long. Sister Yetunde and I unpacked all the luggage. We separated the food items from the clothes and jewelry. We took out all the dried African foods and spread them on a flat tray and surface to dry. Cooking items like crayfish, snails, ground ogbono seeds[22], and dried fishes were spread out to continue drying. The other food items like powdered melon seeds, garri, yam flour, and semolina, were put in their respective containers for storage. I figured that living in America could be challenging for immigrants like us. Unlike Caucasians, we eat different food, and us bringing in food is a cheaper and the only way for us to maintain our African dishes.

Mrs. Babalola and her husband went upstairs to shower and freshen up. Later, they returned downstairs to sit in the adult living room. Auntie Yetunde served her parents. Not long after, her husband entered the house through the kids' living room. I was sitting on one of the chairs in the kitchen when he entered. I curtseyed and bowed my head to greet him; the kids ran to meet

22   Ogbono seeds/soup - Nigerian soup dish with slimy taste. Soup contains many assorted meats and fish.

their father. He just nodded and stared at me. Then, he walked to the adult living room to greet his in-laws. "*E ka bo ma… sir,*" he said, meaning welcome in the Yoruba language. They exchanged greetings. Then, upstairs he went to freshen up.

It was a loud and joyous evening. The adults were in their living room, laughing and talking. The children were running and playing all around the house. The other grandma pulled up a stool and sat in the kitchen against the wall. Not knowing what to do, I sat at the kitchen dining table, watching the children play. This was a very big house; it was a two-story building: upstairs had three bedrooms and a full bathroom. Downstairs was made up of two living rooms= one for the adults and one for the children. It also had a half bathroom, a big dining room, and a kitchen with a dining area. The basement was like a house of its own: It had one bedroom and one living room but no bathroom. The other side of the basement was the laundry room, filled with dirty linens and clothes.

As night approached, everyone found their way to their bed. Mrs. Babalola and her husband took the basement while Mama slept upstairs in one of the rooms with Demola. The girls and I shared the other room while Auntie Yetunde and her husband had their matrimony room, which contained a baby's crib for Raphael. Uncle Amos slept in the living room on the couch. Shockingly, I never thought that I would be sleeping on the bed— three beds in one room. The girls slept on their bunk bed and Kemi and I were on the other mattress. First time for everything.

I lay in bed all night, wondering where I was. Part of me was scared, but the other part wasn't. Mrs. Babalola and her family were here which was a great sense of relief, and that was because they were familiar. On the other hand, I was terrified because it didn't change the situation or the cold shivers I got whenever I see them. *God, please help me*, I silently prayed. Lying there, tears started running down my face. I kept thinking of Mom and home. Although I didn't want to admit it, I missed her. Did she have any idea of what happened or where I was? God, please protect her and watch over me… Dad, I miss you, I thought.

CHAPTER ELEVEN

A LITTLE GLIMPSE OF LIGHT

The next day was a bright and beautiful morning. The sun was out. Oh my gosh, I have overslept. I looked around and noticed that Kemi was still sleeping and when I looked at the mattress, it was soaked with urine. Gross, she had wet the bed. As old as she was, she still peed on herself. I jumped out of bed in a panic. Then quietly and quickly, I made my way downstairs. I knew I was going to get beat up today. Everyone else was up. Auntie Yetunde's husband, Felix, had gone out once again. Mr. and Mrs. Babalola were in their room. I prayed that they were still sleeping. I ran into the kitchen, sitting near the wall, and in the same position was Mama, on the same wooden stool. If I didn't see her go to bed last night, someone would think that she spent the night in that position. I walked up to her and kneeled to greet her. She greeted me back. I took the same seat I had sat in the previous day, looking down and not knowing what to do next. Auntie Yetunde came downstairs later to prepare meals for everyone. When I saw her, I stood up to greet her and then attempted to help her in the kitchen. She insisted that I let her cook and then informed me to have a seat. Mrs. Babalola joined us later in the kitchen. She looked at me and asked why I am not helping my Auntie. I said nothing, but then Auntie Yetunde said she told me I could sit and rest. "Okay," Mrs. Babalola replied.

The next few days went smoothly, but then things went back to normal after about a month. Mrs. Babalola took over the kitchen. She cooked and I helped. A week prior, I was standing by the kitchen sink, handwashing the plates, when I overheard Mrs. Babalola telling her daughter about me in the dining room. "Look, there is nothing that girl cannot do. She can cook, and clean, and you remember she was the one who used to take care of Kemi? Don't let her height fool you," she said in Yoruba. Pretending not to have heard their discussion, I continued to do the dishes. Auntie Yetunde acknowledged her mother. She sounded surprised by her mother's words.

I guessed the comfort was too good to be true. I helped Mrs. Babalola in the kitchen for a while, but now, it was all my responsibility. I did all the house chores, which comprised of cooking, cleaning, doing all laundry, caring for the kids, and serving the adults. I had to bathe and dress the children. Despite it all, I never complained. I didn't get beat these days. Actually, since we landed, they had never put their hands on me. A part of me wondered why, but the other part was sure glad there was no more beating.

In this new country, I have to say they had let a lot of things slide. I remembered when Auntie Yetunde summoned me to call Grandma. The first time calling Mrs. Babalola, "Grandma" was the weirdest thing that will ever come out of my mouth. Shockingly, she didn't say anything but answered. To think of it, I had never called her that before. Usually, she and the husband would yell my name. I would run to them, bow and curtsey, and look down until they ordered me around for errands. These days, their name is Grandma and Grandpa. But these days, all she does is curse at me, insult my mother, and ordered me to get out of her sight. These all hurt also but I was glad beating was not part of it.

After few months passed, and Grandma and Grandpa prepped to leave back to Nigeria. Before they left, Grandma pulled me aside and warned me not to fight. "This country is not a country where you will be fighting, do you hear me? She asked several times until I replied. She then tugged on her right ear and repeats the phrase, "No fighting!" That was her last word before she turned around and left. On the day of her travel, Kemi decided she didn't want to stay, and off she went with them.

The night prior, I overheard Yetunde telling her parents to let me stay. "I'll need someone who can help me around the house," she said. Then, I overheard her telling Grandma to find another help. Having a housemaid is a common practice in Nigeria, unlike in the western world. Many rich and fortunate families will have house help to do all their dirty linens and chores. They'll treat the individuals like a piece of trash while abusing them at the same time. The maid's job is to do whatever she or he has been told, without complaint. As a matter of fact, the wealthy families will expect the maids to be grateful in an attempt to assist her, mostly because they know that the maids had nowhere else to go and their families depend on them. Sadly, they left me here. I was quite sad. I wanted to go back home. I would prefer to be home and close to my birth family than being in a foreign land. Unfortunately, bad things were just meant to happen to me.

In the evening, when Mr. Michael, Yetunde's husband returned, he appeared very displeased. The moment he walked through the door and saw me, his face was not something to talk about. He just looked so angry. He went straight upstairs and started yelling at his wife. Mama went to the first-floor bathroom and locked the door. I think him seeing me here while realizing that Grandma and Grandpa had traveled back to Nigeria really ticked him off. I had always known that he didn't like me since day one. But I understand his anger. In this family, he is the head of the house. His words were final. He should have had an idea of what was going on in his house. In the last few months of being here, I watched his interaction with Grandma. And by the look of things, I can tell that they didn't like each other. Grandma either feared him, or she was just careful not to cause trouble for her daughter. She never wanted to cross his path because whenever he returned home from work, everyone stayed in their lane except for the girls. Although they were more behaved, Mr. Michael either stayed upstairs in his room or went out and returned later. Some other times, Grandma and Grandpa stayed downstairs in the basement to watch TV or to take a nap so that he can have the living room to himself. Anything to avoid each other.

Also, I could tell that Mama and Grandma didn't get along. It seemed like Mama somewhat hates her, but she never said anything. Two in-law rivalries. Mrs. Babalola said a lot of negative stuff about Mama, but Mama never reciprocated. Mama was a quiet grandmother, over 85 years of age, but still very active. She woke up every morning to jog and exercise. She seemed very nice. Mama always prayed, and she sat on her same stool in the kitchen, against the wall. She carried Demola and took care of him. Demola was like her baby. The way she cared for him was like no other, and by the look of things, everyone could tell he was her favorite grandchild. Once in a while, Mama would sit in the children's living room and watch cartoons and then doze off. She was a simple woman, and I like that about her. Mama didn't speak a word of English, but "Hi." She never stepped inside the adult living room even when Grandma and Grandpa were not there. I guessed she figured that was not her place.

Anyways, I stayed downstairs and continued to hear Mr. Michael and Auntie Yetunde talk about me staying back. Later, he came downstairs, sat in the living room, and turned on the television to the news channel. I brought in his dinner, greeted him, and I hurried back into the kitchen. He looked at me and said nothing. Then, Mr. Michael came to the kitchen, grabbed his car keys located inside one of the kitchen cabinets, and drove off. Two days after, Auntie Yetunde drove me to another couple's house and then she left. I never felt so alone in my life.

Here I was, staying with random people that I did not know. I felt so abandoned and unloved. Days passed, and never did I see Auntie Yetunde.

For the next three months, I stayed with Anele's family. They made me feel like a kid for the first time. They had one baby boy named Josh. Mariam, the wife, did everything. Since we didn't know how to communicate, things were quite difficult. Mariam and her husband were Igbo. Igbo is another tribe in Nigeria. Nigeria is comprised of many tribes and languages. To be exact, there are about five hundred and seventy languages in Nigeria. Although we were both Nigerians, we spoke different languages, which made communicating difficult since I didn't understand English.

Living with the couple Anele was quite nice. For once, I felt like a regular kid: eating, sleeping, and watching television. The best part: she helped me braid my hair and even decorated my room. She furnished my room with a comfy bed and stocked the closet with clothes. For the first time in history, I had my own room. Each day before work, Aunt Mariam made food and set mine aside and labeled it breakfasts and lunch. She even got me a Kelly Doll, which became my very best toy. The toy became my very best friend. I felt like a normal kid for a while, even though, deep down, I know things could change within a blink of an eye. But for the main time, I would enjoy myself. While Aunt Mariam and her husband went to work, I stayed home. They told me never to open the door for anyone, and I didn't. Monday through Friday, Josh was taken to daycare, and I stayed home, enjoying myself without worrying about cleaning or cooking.

A few months later, we moved to a new home in Brockton—a five-bedroom, with two bathrooms, and a two kitchens house in Brockton. It was a big house. As always, they warned me not to open doors for anyone. They had their own house key if they needed to enter the house. For the first time ever, I was beginning to like my life. Sometimes, the pastors' kids and I had a sleepover. We took turns sleeping over at each other houses. On weekdays, when the family worked, I watched multiple TV shows and my favorite, the Nickelodeon channel. I loved Nickelodeon cartoons. Watching cartoons like "Hey Arnold," "As Told by Ginger," and "Rocket Power"; are my three all-time favorites. Through these cartoons, I learned how to speak English gradually.

One evening, Aunt Mariam came back from work, and I asked if she wanted water? She looked flustered. "Where did you learn that from?" She asked. I smiled and looked down. She sounded impressed. This was my first statement ever in English. Aunt Mariam was over the moon. Over and over, she asked me to repeat the phrase, and so I did. She spent the evening trying to find out what else I have learned. She was so damned happy and proud of me.

A few months later, she enrolled me at Sun Rays Elementary School. In the beginning, she drove me to school, but later, I learned the route. I discovered the school was only a few minutes' walk if one was taking the back road. I was used to walking in Nigeria. I walked everywhere. So, this was no big deal. Going to school was challenging. Being the new kid was not fun. As my English improved, I learned that I am the African kid that students mock. I was the African kid who apparently looks like a monkey? First time in my life, I felt worthless and ugly. So, this was what these kids thought of me. I never considered myself pretty, but the student made sure I felt worst about myself. I never realized that my skin color was that awful. Gradually on the inside, part of me wished to be white or fair in complexion. Being fair in complexion was better than having brown skin. For the first time, I started to realize that colors matter. In this part of the world, skin color does matter more than anything else. In Nigeria, colorism is something I never had to think about. Most everyone looked the same in one way or the other. There is no I am better or prettier than you because I am lighter in complexion. For this, I realized how much I miss Nigeria.

Recess was the worst part of going to school. While everyone played, I sat there watching. I sat in a corner, all alone. No one ever invited me to join them. Everyone made fun of me, most especially David. David Joseph is the worst black guy I ever met. All he did was make fun of me and call me a dummy. I understood that I did not know how to speak English well, but it didn't justify his cruelty towards me. I felt that the fact we were both blacks should count for something, but in this case, it meant nothing to him. In my class, there were only three black students—David, Ariana, and me. I supposed the two of them were born here because they had clear speech and no accents. Ariana was nice, though. During indoor recess, she tended to play with me. We played with Legos and other building blocks. Other times, we played tic tac toe or Jenga. Sometimes, Nicole—a Caucasian girl with brunette hair and blue eyes, joined us to play. She was very nice too. I loved her eyes. They were blue like the sea. Each time the girls talked, I couldn't help but stare at their lips to watch how they articulated their words. I listened to their dictions.

Every day, I went home with sadness in my heart. When I was in Nigeria, I was the best in my class. Now, all I did was lay in bed each night, thinking of how David and others kept calling me a monkey. Every now and then, I would look at my skin and compare it to theirs. David and Arianna did have slender, pointier noses, while my nose is flat with huge nostrils. I couldn't change my skin tone. This was how God created me. When I thought of this, my heart felt heavy. After my long deep thoughts, I looked up to God. I knew that God was my salvation and my strength. I remembered the words of the Bible, saying, "Sadness may endure for a night, but joyous cometh in the morning." Thus, I prayed:

Heavenly Father, please put a smile on my face and heal this inferiority complex that I am feeling within me. I know that you created me in Your own image, so please, God, teach me to love and accept my skin. In spite of everything, I have to keep my head up. Tomorrow will be a better day; it has to be.

CHAPTER TWELVE:
THE YEAR OF STRUGGLE

During my six months of living with Aunt Mariam, I started feeling at home. I started calling her mom. I thought she liked it. She never complained. Neither did her husband. Unfortunately, I couldn't bring myself to call her husband Dad. It just didn't sound right. I usually referred to him as 'sir" when needed. Then a month later, I didn't know what happened, but I noticed things started to change.

First, Uncle Tayo showed up at our doorstep one day to ask for Grandma's home number. I thought it was weird, but at this time, I can still vividly remember the house number, so I gave it to him. Then randomly, as the weeks went by, each Sunday I noticed that Auntie Yetunde and her kids started attending the same church with us——Christian Church of God. Each Sunday got weirder and weirder. My gut feeling told me something was wrong, and I think there must have been an altercation between the two friends. Whatever happened between them, things started to change for the worse.

It was so weird seeing Yetunde, her kids, husband, and Mama in church. I didn't know how to react whenever I saw them, but as always, when they called me, I answered and curtseyed to greet them. The altercation must have been very bad. Gradually, I noticed Aunt Mariam and her husband's bad attitude toward me. She started making me do all the house chores. I began cooking and cleaning the entire house once again. Aunt Mariam did have a big heart, though. She pretended to hate me, but deep down, I knew she didn't. She couldn't help but help me whenever I was cleaning.

One Wednesday evening, Auntie Yetunde came to our house to drag me out. She took me back to her house. Aunt Mariam stood and watched. On Sunday of the same week, Mr. Anele showed up at the church. He shouted my name and I ran to him. He told me to let go and then pulled my hair. I was so confused and started crying. I think pulling my hair was an accident and he intended to try to pull my right arm. We made it out of the church, and the church members rushed out to witness the scene. Some people stood and gossiped while others shouted for him to let me go. I turned around, and Auntie Yetunde was behind me. She grabbed me by my jacket and ordered me to get in the car. After that Sunday, that was it.

Before I could say anything, I was back living with Auntie Yetunde. I wished someone would have asked me what I wanted. Being back with Auntie Yetunde, a few weeks later, I overheard the conversation about how

Aunt Mariam was almost done completing my adoption papers. I could not believe she wanted to adopt me and make me her daughter. Seriously, how I wished, she had. I would have loved to be her daughter. She enrolled me in school, took care of my needs, and most importantly, she showed me love and affection. She was an awesome woman. And every now and then, I think of her.

When Grandma heard about it in Nigeria, she wasn't too happy. Things turned out for the worse, and now I was back with Yetunde's family. After the embarrassing arguments displayed in the church, Aunt Mariam and Josh never came back to church. That was the end of their friendship.

It had been a long journey up to this point, most notably with the back-and-forth movement. It seemed like no one cared about me or my feelings. Poor girls like me don't have choices. It will take a miracle to break free from this bondage of poverty. Moving back with Yetunde was tougher than ever. I guess I was used to the nice treatment. I was used to Aunt Mariam and me going through the drive-through to order burgers and fries from the fast-food restaurant. Hmmm...I loved the fast-food joints near the house. I loved French fries, most especially when served hot. Within a few days, reality set back in. I became the housemaid once again.

After the church drama, things were a riot at first, but soon everything died down. The family had to keep up appearances. They enrolled me in school with their daughters at Brockton Elementary, located on Pearls Street. Before starting school, unspoken rules and regulations were established. And of course, I already knew what to expect. Nobody needed to tell me what to do before I did it. I was the house-help and this was an expectation. It was my responsibility to juggle both the schoolwork and the house chores together. There was nothing I had not done. The good news I can say was that I didn't get beaten anymore. Actually, since landing here, beating was far from my punishment. It was insults. Eating was not a problem. I cooked enough for everyone. Once everyone was done eating, I served myself. Because my English had gotten better, going to school was much better. Auntie Yetunde never commended me on my English-speaking ability. But it was whatever. Once again, I was back in my element, going to school to keep the sadness away.

Starting a new school was not pleasant. It had been months, and although I did not make any friends, I tried as much as possible not to let it bother me. The students there were awful humans. They often made fun of my accent whenever I spoke, and for this reason, I hated my accent. I hated it more than anything. The teasing and bullying made me shy away from social gatherings, or anything that had to do with me reading aloud, both in class or the public. I remember losing a math game just because of my accent. We were indoors playing with multiplication flashcards, and apparently, my number forty sounds like fourteen. When I explained myself, the students claimed not to have understood what I said. Too much peer pressure and the feeling of needing to belong.

Being the new African in town, I didn't get a lot of welcome at first. I didn't know whether it was curiosity or just plain being ignorant, but most white students will ask questions such as, "Does everyone in Africa walk naked?

Are lions and tigers roaming on the street?" By the way they talked, they seem to believe Africa is a jungle: a place where people have no water and no houses. Jerry, a Caucasian guy, came next to me at recess one of the days and asked if I lived in a hut in Africa, and why do I not have a round belly like the kids on TV? At first, I was mad because these people think Africa is a dumping ground, but as I grow older, I learned to believe the questions were out of curiosity and lack of knowledge. These people think Africa is one community rather than a continent. Despite the outrageous demeaning questions, I clarified all their curiosities, with the exception of lions and tigers roaming the streets. Some of the students think this is "cool," so why should I change their perception about it? For once, it was not bad to think Africa is a cool place.

Not fitting in anywhere was my daily struggle, but I preferred to be at school than at home on any given day. The first year was challenging. I was quiet, and I stayed in my lane, avoiding drama at all costs. The only drama in school was the inferiority complex of the idea that being white was better than black, and the worst of all, being African is worse than being black American. Nigeria was never like that because skin color doesn't matter. The only thing that matters in Nigeria is "wealth." Facing silent racism is something new to me. Once, Mrs. Daniels, our sixth-grade substitute teacher, kept all the black students in the classroom, including me, in detention while she allowed the whites to go outside to have recess. Her sending me to detention was the highlight of her low-key racism towards black students. When you think about it, when is it a crime to do homework during free time? I was done with my classwork and to keep myself busy, I took out my homework and begin working on it. I never knew that calls for detention, but that was her reason.

After two years at Brockton Elementary, I still stayed to myself. I smiled more often, but that was mainly at school. After a while, I blended in with my peers. My accent was not as thick as it used to be, and people could finally understand me without the "what?" And "huh?" when I spoke. Finally, students got to know me, but they only knew me as "the smart" and "quiet" kid. I could tell by the way they looked at me that they admired my intelligence. Every time we did spelling or math, they usually wanted to be on my team. I discovered that I am very competitive. Education and being smart was the only thing that I had to fall back on. James and I were very competitive. James was our next class neighbor, and a white Caucasian male. James was the best in his class, and I was the best in mine. We competed against each other, but I liked him. We brought out the best in each other. With James and I being competitive, I have to say he brought out the positive side of me. Similar to when I was in Nigeria, most of my teachers admired my intelligence and my thirst for learning. I became more than an African kid. The positivity motivated me to work harder and be the best in everything I did. Teachers encouraged me to compete in competitions.

Like math, I also loved physical education. I was very good at running. One day, James and I were practicing for the school's yearly competition, and during our practice, we collided and tumbled over each other, causing both of us to scrape our knees and arms on the hard pavement. We were injured, and the gym teacher sent us to the nurse's office to get treated. Every year, the school selected its best runners to compete in the triathlon, a competition whereby all the schools gathered to compete with one another. The best school won the giant trophy. It was discovered that James and I were the best runners. In the end, I was selected to run the 400-meter dash while James was selected for the other parts. Unfortunately, our school did not win, but I had a great time competing with other students.

Living with Auntie Yetunde and her family was every adopted child's nightmare. The school was my salvation and escape route from the turmoil at home. I did exceptionally well in school, and I was proud of myself for that. Unfortunately, that was not the case for her daughters. Each time, their grades came out, I got the blame for not helping them. Auntie Yetunde and Grandma would say I didn't help them enough. For some reason, I didn't understand why it was my fault for their children's failures. I did all I could to assist, which included teaching them their homework and sometimes, doing it for them. That was the only way I could get to sleep at the end of the night. If they didn't finish, it was my responsibility to finish the rest. While Auntie Yetunde got upset, the husband was actually happy for me. He always praised me for a job well done on my report card. For some reason, Auntie Yetunde's behaviors were harsh. I didn't know whether it was because I was doing better in school, but she became a horrific human being. The knowledge of her coming to the house scared the heck out of me. I didn't know who was worse, her or her mother. Like mother like daughter—that is how the saying goes anyway. I have to say I am not that surprised about her attitude.

Similar to Grandpa, the husband never said anything. Mr. Michael was a registered nurse, working in a rehab hospital and starting his career track toward becoming a nurse practitioner. Yetunde was a licensed vocational nurse (LVN), who worked at a nursing home. Since I moved back into the house, the husband was another story. He looked at me with eyes that didn't betray his emotions. I didn't understand him. When he was home, I felt the tension between us, but I didn't know whether it was in my head. But when he was around me, he got quiet, and he watched me. After a while, I ignored this awkward feeling. I thought I was being paranoid. Things between him and I were okay after many months, so I let my guard down. Mr. Michael was somewhat nice. He was the only adult in the house who talked to me. For the first time, I felt like I had a father or father-like figure. He surely made me feel like a human. He never scolded me, but instead celebrated my success. He always told me how he was proud of me, most especially when it involved school. He told me how he admired my determination. "You are a hard-worker, Auntie Dami," he would say. Hearing this made me feel good. Sometimes, he would tap me on my shoulder for a well job done, and other times, he would attempt to hug me. My mom had never hugged me, so the idea of a hug seems abnormal. I grew up in Nigeria where giving hugs are not common, most especially not to strangers or housemaids. After a while, I started calling him Daddy, mainly because that was what everyone calls him. Calling him Uncle, Mr. Michael, and, or Ashley's or Renee's dad just seemed awkward. It just felt like I had to call him that too.

This was what I thought until one Sunday night, two months after my tenth birthday. Auntie Yetunde was at work, the kids were sleeping, and I prepping for the next day. I was working downstairs, cleaning up for the night. When I finished, I went upstairs to iron everyone's clothes. Mr. Michael called me into his room. I dropped everything, hurried to his door, and knocked on the door. He ordered me to come in. I cracked the door open and looked inside. The room was dark. The glare from the hallway light shined through the room, and I noticed Mr. Michael was in his white bath towel. In my mind, it felt like something bad was about to happen. Standing near the door, he ordered me to come inside. "Come take these clothes. I need it for work," he said. On his ironing table were his faded blue top scrub, a white inner t-shirt, and a cream color dress pants.

I hesitated for a while. Something didn't feel right. In my head, I keep wondering why the room is dark. I then took a step inside the room and headed to grab his clothing. He then approached me and closed the door behind me. He grabbed my wrist tightly and pulled me closer to his chest. My heart sunk to my chest. The only emotion I felt was fear. I couldn't shout or yell but instead was at a standstill. My heart continued to beat faster than ever before. He whispered in my ears and said, "Auntie Dami? Do you know that you are very beautiful?" I stayed silent. My mouth was muted and my body instantly was paralyzed. "You know I can make all this go away. I can give your mom money so she can take care of herself. What do you say? How about two hundred thousand Naira? That is a lot of money. She needs money to care for your sisters. Your mother really needs help. Think about it. Think about your mother and your sisters. You know they are really counting on you." he continued.

I stood there in silence and tears began rolling down my eyes. His body pressed against mine. "You know, I've wanted you for a long time. You're such a pretty girl, Auntie Dami," he added. The next thing, he picked me up and threw me on his bed, and I landed face down. I tried sliding off the bed: my upper body on the bed but my feet barely touching the hard-wooden floor. Then he moved closer. The more I struggled, the more force he used. He ripped off my clothes, broke my necklace as he grabbed my neck, and then began kissing it. Terrified as I was, he stuck his tongue down my throat. He then turned me around, twisted my arms, and pinned them behind me.

Breathing heavily, he said, "You should stop struggling." I slid to the ground, and he plopped his whole body on me and pinned my arms above my head. He then inserted his penis inside of me. *Man… it hurts*. All I felt was the pain. When he finished, he released my arms. I ran to the bathroom and locked the door. I stood there crying. I looked down my leg, and there was blood. My elbows and knees were scraped from the hardwood floor. I continued to cry while cleaning myself. When I finished, I unlocked the bathroom door, and there he was, standing at the door. I dashed off, passing his side, into the children's room to continue ironing the clothes.

RESILIENCE

After this event, my soul was not the same. I cried for days. Each night, I lay in bed thinking of the horror of what had happened. I still could not make up for what had happened. Who do I tell? Who would believe me? Auntie Yetunde had never treated me like her daughters. Her parents hated me. So, calling them to inform them would be a waste of time. Also, the children don't know anything. Renee and Ashley were too young to comprehend the situation that I am battling. I couldn't even say what happened. I bled for days. Covering what happened and wearing toilet tissues in my underwear. Sometimes, I sneaked inside Auntie Yetunde's room to steal her pantiliners. One evening, I was in the bathroom, when she walked up to me and handed me some of her pads. "This is for 'period', stick it to your underwear. There are more in the room," she said. I thanked her and she walked away.

Each nightfall became a nightmare. I hated it when it got dark outside. The whole event played in my head repeatedly. I couldn't sleep or eat. Every time I closed my eyes, it was the same reoccurring nightmare. Despite everything, I continued to do all the work in the house. The cooking, cleaning, laundry, and taking care of the kids. Auntie Yetunde's attitude didn't help the situation and at the sight of her, I was more infuriated. She was supposed to be a mother and she was hardly here. Since the event, I wished she was home, but unfortunately, her attitudes were something I could not tolerate. In this situation, I was the mother, and she was the teenage kid. When she was not working, all she did was go out to hang out with her friends or go shopping at the mall. I don't know if I preferred her being there to not. In the house, it was just the kids and I. Mama was home, but she was just an old woman. She didn't do much but eat and sleep.

A few weeks later, I was cooking when Mr. Michael stood by me and said, "If you think of telling someone, no one will believe you. If you just agree to doing this, Auntie Dami, I'll make your life so much easier. Think of your mom and your sisters. They all depend on you. You are in America, everyone's favorite place. Do you know how lucky you are? Do you know many people wish they were here, in your shoes?" In my head, I knew I was in hell. The fact is, I never wanted to be here. And, so far, this country had not done me justice. As he spoke, I ignored him and continued to do the dishes. Walking away, he mumbled, "You are so stubborn." As he walked away, I couldn't help but burst into tears, clearing my eyes after each teardrop.

Eight weeks after the first incident, another event happened. This time, Mr. Michael took the kids out to play. He dropped them at the park with Mama and then returned to the house. Auntie Yetunde was at work once again. When I heard the parking of the car but no sounds of the children, I ran into hiding. He spent hours searching through the house while calling my name. He searched until he found me in the basement. There I was underneath the bed in Grandma's old room. He dragged me out, threw me on the bed, and pinned my hands above my head. When he finished, he drove back out to pick up the children. I cleaned myself up and got back to work, fearful of what might happen if Auntie Yetunde returned from her lunch break. The last thing I wanted was for her to start yelling about how slow I was in prepping her meal.

A few weeks later, the same thing occurred again. It happened over and over again, and after a while, it was like nothing. I focused on school and maintained my grades. Graduating sixth grade from Brockton Elementary School was like an ordinary day, but I was excited. On the morning of graduation, I woke up like always, got the kids ready for school, and went to school afterward, wearing my black and beige faded color dress. The school day was an exciting one. Every student gathered in a joyous mood, laughing, and discussing how their parents would be at their graduation. I looked at everyone's graduation outfits, and they was beautiful. Watching all the students, I knew they are anxiously waiting to reunite with their parents. As I watched everyone, deep down, I was sad but hopeful. I was hopeful because it was Tuesday morning, and Auntie Yetunde didn't work.

Tuesday was always her off day. Sometimes, she would pick up the early shift, but most times, she was off. So, I hoped she would come to show her support for my accomplishment. By mid-morning, my graduating class was ready to walk down the aisle. We filed into a single line and onto the field where we will be called to receive our certificate. I looked over the crowd, many families standing and some in their seats, applauding as the program began. Throughout the program, I kept my eyes on the lookout, hoping by fate to see Auntie Yetunde among the crowded parents, but in the end, nothing. After the ceremony, many kids got dismissed and went home with their families, while I stayed back in the classroom. Staying in the classroom, I couldn't help but feel sad and embarrassed. I wished I had someone to show their support for me. After a long thought, I blamed myself for being optimistic; hoping for "just maybe," she would show; an expectation that comes crashing right before my eyes. After all, I was not her daughter. After school, I walked home to continue my daily task. I walked into the house, and it was like nothing had happened. Nobody in the entire house wished me congratulations except Mr. Michael. In private, he wished me well for a job well done and for making straight A's in my academics. Although I felt his sincerity, I couldn't help but feel hurt at the same time. That day, I learned that expectation brings hurts and disappointment. After a while, I let my mind be at ease.

I looked at Mr. Michael and nod in acknowledgement to his words. I thanked him for his kind words, and then continued with my task. I seriously hated this man and hated living in with them. His support for my education meant nothing. One minute he was comforting me, and the next minute, his sexual urges took control. The more my body matured, the more Auntie Yetunde called me a prostitute, and her husband found me more sexually appealing. For these reasons, I hated my body. I hated my boobs and my developing body parts. Raping me had become his hobby. Two or sometimes three times a month, he would have his way with me. It was sad to say, but I was getting pretty used to it. As the years passed, it just seems like a normal thing. Rape meant nothing to me. I learned that fighting didn't stop the monster. I also learned that the more I struggled, the more aggressive he got. So, I asked myself, why fight or argue.

On days I allowed him to get his way, he was nice. He went out shopping, buying me new clothes. Sometimes, he claimed he sent my mom money, but who knows if that is really true. Other times, he would take me and the girls shopping and tell me to pick anything I want. The only reason he took the girls along was to cover his tracks so his wife would not find out that he was doing me a favor. The only problem was Auntie Yetunde ended up asking me who bought this and that. At times, she might ask, "Where did you get this?" Other times, she stayed silent, pretending she didn't notice the new clothes but then made a living in the house unbearable. I could tell her husband buying clothes for me disturbed her. She would take her anger on me and continue calling me fat and a prostitute.

For months, the words "prostitute and fat" reigned in my head, but I tried not to let it bother me, even though I knew that I was lying to myself. I began covering my body from my neck to my toes when going out to prevent any unwanted attention. The one thing that stood out to me was how I hated my body and, in the end, I became conscious of my body. Sometimes, I forced myself to vomit after eating. Dami, you don't want to be fat; I'd tell myself.

To ease the pain of being called a prostitute, I gave Ashley and Renee the clothes their father bought. When Auntie Yetunde saw the clothes on her daughters, she never seemed to complain, she instead complimented Ashley, saying, "She looked like a model." It just seemed like it was okay for her daughters to wear the clothes. But if I wore them, it was an abomination. She was astounded by Ashley's beauty. They all hoped that one day, she would be a model because she was slim, tall, and fairer in complexion, just like her mom. Renee, on the other hand, was more of a simple girl who hated wearing heels. She was dark like her dad, and of an average height. Renee could be described as a tomboy while Ashley is the complete opposite. She loved fashion. Auntie Yetunde liked to dress up her daughters. She made them wear expensive jewelry around their necks, most especially on Sundays, while she gave me oversized clothes to wear to church. Despite it all, I tried not to focus on that. I know I was stuck in this messed-up world, but I had to live my best life. My mother's teaching kept flickering in my head, saying that I should always know the daughter of whom I was. All I did was pray that God should send me a helper and a friend.

As the rape continued, I started sleeping in my jeans and belt to reduce his accessibility. Sometimes, I even slept with a knife underneath my pillow. These provided me with a little sense of security. His phrase, "You are so stubborn," played in my mind, but I did not care. I told myself that if I had to sleep with a knife underneath my pillow, it would be worth it. Not long after, God's word came into my mind, saying it was a sin to kill. *God will never forgive me if I commit a murder,* I thought I could go to jail for my murderous action. I didn't have the strength for that. I thought of taking my own life but killing myself or him wouldn't solve anything. I imagined how my mom would feel if she heard that I was dead. I didn't want to cause her pain, besides, I still remembered the pain in her eyes, when she lost Dad and how she could not do anything for months. I began to have an internal struggle; an internal battle of not knowing what to do, and the repercussions.

After those long devastating thoughts, I stopped placing knives underneath my pillow. I learned to accept my faith in the house. One year, two years, and three years passed, and the same situations continued. One of the days, Mr. Michael walked up to me while I was in the kitchen cooking.

"Meet me in the basement tonight," he said. I nodded. When the night appeared, I sent the children to bed, and I began prepping for the next day. Around 10:30 P.M, I went to the basement to meet with him. He was sitting in the living room where Grandma and Grandpa usually sat. He told me to have a seat, and I did, then he said, "You know if you cooperate, I'll start your papers. You need papers in this country, and as of right now, you don't. If you cooperate, I'll start filing for your green card. The choice is yours". He walked towards me, stroked my face and hair with his hand, and then pulled down his pants. His penis was sticking out. I turned my head and closed my eyes. Then I looked back at him. Whether I agreed or not, he was going to get his way. I sat still. He got to his knees and told me to lie flat. I watched him unbuckle my belt, unzip my jeans, and pull down my pants. He then got up and climbed on me. I laid there while he got his way. I listened to him grunting and moaning, his sweat dripping on my face, and when he finished, he got up.

"Your p*** is so sweet, Auntie Dami. Did you put sugar in there?" he said, breathing heavily and laughing at the same time. "Don't you think it is better to give it to me than to those small boys out there? They can't do anything for you," he continued. "I'll take care of you. Your mom, your sisters… anything you want. You don't want to give it to those small boys for free," He added.

He looked at me, but I pretended not to hear him. I laid there stiff and emotionless. Surprisingly he didn't ejaculate on me but instead on the carpet. Normally, he would do this on my body or face, but it's different this time. Maybe, it was because I didn't struggle, or maybe it was because he knew my menstrual cycle is about to start. Quite to say, this man knew me well and knew my menstrual cycle. I loved my cycle because it availed me a week of no sex. Well, not only that, each time Grandma and Grandpa arrived from Nigeria, there was a reduction in the number of sexual advances. Grandma and Grandpa visiting had become a blessing. Honestly, the best and the worst part of the year was seeing them both in the house. I couldn't stand Grandma, but her presence limited Mr. Michael's attempts.

Every one to two years, they spent about three to four months then traveled back. Their three to four months of vacation spent in America felt like an eternity of torture for many of us in the house. Renee and Ashley hated the fact that Grandma was lazy. They have called Grandma lazy on multiple occasions, but I didn't blame them for their reasoning. I'm glad someone else thought she was annoying. Grandma was crap and a difficult person to please. This woman could be watching television in the living room; then, she would call someone who was upstairs to come to turn on the television or for someone to hand her the TV remotes that were within arm's length away from her. The same thing went for the house phone and every other thing. As for Mama, the two grandmothers never got along. They were like two strangers living in the house. Once Grandma arrived, Mama left to stay with her other son so that she could find peace.

As for the kids' father, a month of no sex was hell for him not to speak of three months. In whatever ways, he had to find excuses to get me out of the house. Any chance he could get, he jumped at it. Sometimes, he would tell everyone that I had to help him in the other house. Mr. Michael owned a few houses in Brockton. He rented these houses to tenants, and each time a tenant moved out, we spend the whole day cleaning up the place. Actually, he cleaned, and I helped, but in the end, he got his way. Other times, he just brought me to the house to have sex. Once he was done, he would take me back to the house. The tenants' house was always his escape route. Sometimes, he lied about going to the car auction, and other times he wanted me to accompany him to Chelsea, a city located in Suffolk County, Massachusetts. Returning from the road trip, he would pull over at a motel, park his car in the back, and take me in to have his way with me. Mr. Michael would lie about anything, just to get me alone.

Riding with Mr. Michael was the worst and sickening. I watched him cat-call and whistle at young high school girls who were walking on the sidewalk—talking about no respect for women. This man even whistled at girls in front of his kids. Ashley usually said, "Daddy, why are you doing that?" Renee never said anything, likewise the boys, Demola, and Raphael. They usually smiled, stayed quiet, and then looked at their sisters. I hoped they don't become like their father in the future.

One of the days, when he finished climaxing, I asked if he would ever do this to any of his daughters. "Of course not. That's blood," he replied. I had to ask him because the girls and I were only a few years apart. Since he said, "No," I kept quiet, got up, and went back to cleaning.

The stress of living there was indescribable. On two different occasions, I fainted while cleaning and cooking. The first time I ever fainted, I didn't know what was happening. All I remembered was that I felt light-headed, and then I developed chills. The next thing I remembered after this was waking up on the kitchen floor, covered in sweat. I figured that I passed out. It was sad to say that I was on the floor for however long with no one to help. Two months after the first episode, the second episode of fainting happened. This time, I began experiencing the same symptoms of chills, diaphoretic, and lighthead-edness. I made my way upstairs, and the moment I got to the room, I collapsed. I was conscious, but my body was paralyzed. I couldn't move my legs or arms. I tried opening my eyes, but my head and the room were spinning. I closed my eyes until the spinning stopped. Like the first time, I lay there, covered in sweat, and waited for my symptoms to pass. Once everything subsided, I went back to cleaning and acted as if nothing had happened.

CHAPTER FOURTEEN

THE BETRAYAL

When I was fifteen, and towards the end of junior high school at West Middle School, I met a guy named Tobi in church. It was after church service on a Sunday afternoon. He walked past me, and I was blown away.

The first thing I noticed was how he dressed, followed by his Ralph Lauren Polo cologne. He was dressed in a grey suit, a light purple collar shirt, and brown shoes. Tobi was a talented guy with a fantastic voice. Listening to him sing on that Sunday, my mouth dropped. He not only sang, but he played the drums and the piano. I had to say he was good looking. I couldn't help but stare at him. I watched until he was out of sight. Tobi was nineteen years old, and five feet, seven inches tall. He was dark in complexion with a handsome low-cut hairstyle.

Since I met Tobi, Sunday church services had become more interesting. I was head over heels with a crush on him. Although he hardly noticed me at first, gradually I made my appearance known to him. After service on one of the Sundays, he walked over to me and said hi.

From there, our friendship began. I thought I might like someone for the very first time.

For the next couple of years, Tobi and I became closer. Getting to know him made the last few months of junior high easier. I was used to the ill treatment but meeting a guy like him made things better. All of a sudden, the punishments didn't seem so bad. Within a few months, I disclosed everything about my life and everything happening in the house. Tobi was compassionate. He understood me. I knew he was disturbed by my situation and became angry at the Adesanya family. He wished he could do something, but in this case, he was powerless. He told me he was on a student visa. I figured him being on a visa meant he didn't want to get in the crossfire with the drama. So, he shared his personal story about his childhood and how he once got molested by his mom's friends. I felt for him. Listening to his story gave me encouragement and hope. It made me feel like I was not alone, and most importantly, I had someone to talk to and relate to.

I had grown so close to Tobi that he had become my only trusted friend and boyfriend. We started dating secretly. Dating Tobi was the best. He showed me love and he always bought me perfumes and Nike sneakers. Tobi had good taste in fashion and in dressing. Although he hardly worked, his monthly allowance came from his parents who resided in Nigeria. Tobi's parents were somewhat doing well. They were not wealthy, but also not poor. That's why they could afford to send him abroad to study. Each time he bought me something, he also bought the girls something to erase suspicions and protect our relationship. Tobi made me happy.

Since I met him, walking in severe weather to school was less of a thing. Sometimes, he dropped me off, and other times I walked. I remembered walking to West Middle School, on a rainy day; Auntie Yetunde dropped off her children while she left me to walk in the rain. Luckily for me, I met a strange Black American man that day. I called him my guardian angel. The man was driving his dark grey sedan car when he saw me. He saw me, pulled his car over to the right, and then yelled across the street to get my attention. I looked up and crossed the street. Then, he opened his car door. Standing and looking into his eyes, I hesitated for a few minutes while the rain beat down on me. I entered the car slowly and sat down. The strange man gave me a ride to school. I know the first rule of life is to avoid strangers. I don't know why I got into a stranger's car, but for some reason, I wasn't scared, a voice inside me kept telling me that I could trust him. Besides, what was the worst possible thing that could happen that I was not already dealing with? This man was God-sent. He was pleasant. He kept reassuring me throughout the car ride that he has four daughters and he would never do anything to hurt them or me. I looked at him and I didn't say anything. The man dropped me off in front of my school, handed me a change of clothes, and then drove off. I took the clothes and headed straight to the girls' bathroom. I guessed it was one of his daughters' clothes.

Although I walked the same path every day since day one, I never saw him again. Every day, I kept my eyes on the road, hoping and praying that I would see my guardian angel. I wished I could see him again to thank him for his kind gesture and return his clothes. I kept the clothes inside my locker, and eventually, at the end of the school year, I had to throw them out.

So, since then, Tobi had been my occasional helper and comforter. On Sunday after church, while Auntie Yetunde was at her workers' meetings, Tobi and I hung outside the church. We sat and talked all day until it was time to go home. Auntie Yetunde really hated that I was becoming close to Tobi. She hated Tobi socializing with me. My socializing gave her more reasons to call me a prostitute, but I didn't care. One day, she placed a call to my mother in Nigeria and told her that all I did was follow boys. Mom was so upset, and she started shouting at me. Not even a "Hi." She just went straight to yelling and shouting. I attempted to tell her about what had been happening, but she didn't want to hear it. Instead, she continued to shout. Listening to her voice, I became emotional and started to cry. Oh, I haven't cried in a long time. After listening to her yell, she told me to be good and well behaved, and before I could answer her, Auntie Yetunde grabbed the phone from my ear. I thought I would never hear my mom's voice again. Hearing her voice brought back memories. Oh, I missed her. I missed her a lot. She continued talking with my mom and by the way my mom sounded, I was pretty sure she was begging and pleading for me.

I laid in bed that night, thinking about Mom and what she had said. For weeks, I was devastated by the fact that she didn't want to hear me out. Her scolding reminded me of our last conversation and the unfortunate events that had happened in the past. Lying in bed, I was bitterly angry once again. The memories came rushing in like a flood. Her shouting and yelling that she didn't ask me to send her money kept playing in my mind. I would have thought that after all my hard work and determination to better support her, she would say thank you for the assistance. Instead, all she did was yell at me for trying to support the family. I felt like if I could save some money for her, she wouldn't have to keep going to the Babalola's house and keep begging them for assistance. It hurt to keep hearing Mrs. Babalola calling my mom a beggar. It was the worst reminder of how poor my family was. So, I worked hard for the money I earned. I saved every dollar and pennies that I could.

To earn money, I recycled every alcohol bottle and soda can I found. It took many months of gathering before I recycled them in exchange for some cash. With five to six hefty black trash bags, I usually made about thirty to fifty dollars. To generate more money, I helped Auntie Yetunde's friends and acquaintances cook for Nigerian parties. Cooking for the parties, I generated about one hundred twenty dollars in profits. Unfortunately, I had to split the money evenly with her daughters even though they were not of help. They hardly did anything and splitting the money with Ashley and Renee drove me insane, but something was better than nothing. In the end, all they did was spend all their money on candy and goodies until there was nothing left. The sad and annoying part was that after months of saving all the money, Auntie Yetunde would borrow it and never pay me back.

To make matters worse, asking her for it was impossible because it is not our nature or culture. Asking parents to pay up the debts they owe you is considered disrespectful. They'll make someone feel guilty because they claim it is because of them you are alive. They claim that they've given you life, food, and shelter, and for this reason, you should be more grateful. I think the worst part of giving her my money was that she used it for unnecessary things.

I remember the day my three hundred and sixty dollars went missing, after lying about not having money to lend her. When I discovered that the money was gone, it was difficult to bring myself to tell Auntie Yetunde the truth. I asked the girls but they both denied seeing it. That day, I regretted lying to Auntie Yetunde about not having the money when she wanted to borrow it. Unfortunately, asking the kids led to their mother finding out, and in the end, I got in trouble. All Auntie Yetunde could say was, "I thought you said that you don't have any money, and if not, where did you get the money?" I looked at her and didn't answer. Deep down, I know I couldn't have answered her. After her scolding, all she could call me was selfish. After the incident, she told her mom, who then placed a call to my mother and told her that all I do is lie. Once again, all mom did was yell and shout.

Since that day, I regretted trying to send her money. I regretted placing the money inside the written letter. I never expected that Grandma and Grandpa would open up the envelope and read my letter and then take the money. I thought by doing this, I was being smart. But again, I would have never thought of such an idea, if

Grandma and Grandpa have been honest in giving my mom the money I worked hard to save. It took me a while, but I learned that they usually give her partial or sometimes none of the money. But when I thought about it, the family never seems to surprise me with their crooked ways. They are selfish and greedy. Sending money to my mom through them was like placing a fish tray in front of a cat and telling the cat not to eat the fish.

After weeks of being upset and angry; at first, I promised myself that I would never send money to Mom again. I hated her lack of appreciation and her tendency of being too weak to stand up for anything. She was too softminded, and the odd part was that she thought God was going to solve this issue. Even though the Bible said that we should cast all our burdens to God, I still believed this maltreatment wouldn't end until Mom developed the guts to defend herself and her kids. In the end, even though I wanted to blame her, I couldn't. I blamed myself for feeling bad and for wanting to help. I hated Grandma for calling her a beggar, and Mr. Michael for flaunting his wealth to feel empowered. But I did pray that God would give me the strength to withstand these people and their oppressions. I tried to see the best of her in the long run. I told myself it was not her fault. I let myself believe that her emotional outburst was a result of what she had been told. I tried to reassure myself that was okay, but at the same time, I wished she could understand me. I wished she would listen to me for once.

The last thing I wanted was to disappoint Mom. No matter what, I love her, and I wanted to make her smile and get her out of poverty. I told myself that I was going to make her proud because I know that Tobi was a great distraction from the daily oppression. And I would never let my love for him prevent me from reaching my goal. From that day forward, instead of talking with Tobi on Sunday, we decided to act like we didn't know each other in public. Sneaking around was the new normal. Sometimes, he would meet me after school to hang out. Other times, he would pick me up and take me to his apartment. He would encourage me to rest my head and take a nap before dropping me off near the house.

As I promised myself, I finished the remaining school year with all A's. Graduating from middle school was exciting and a great sense of achievement. I won many awards and trophies for being the best. I even impressed David Joseph and his friends, who looked up to me as the smart kid. In his mind, he was probably dumbfounded because I was that girl he used to bully and tease for not knowing how to speak good English. But in my mind, I never thought I would see him again once I left Sun Rays Elementary. I guessed this is what you call a small world or small community.

I started high school in the fall of 2009. High School Massachusetts was a massive high school containing over 4,000 diverse students, not including teachers and staff. The school was like a campus, divided into four main academic buildings with red, green, yellow, and blue colors. These colors allowed students to navigate through the school to get to their next class. My homeroom was in the red building, but all my classes were in all the other color buildings except for red.

Entering high school gave me a sense of hope. Just four more years, then I'm off to college. My number one goal was to move to the farthest college once I graduated. The farther the school, the better. In the meantime, I needed to stay focused: I needed to focus on my AP and Honor classes. I need grants and scholarships if I plan on going to college. With scholarships, I could attend the best colleges, become a medical doctor, and finally turn my life around. People always say education is life. This is the only way to get out of poverty and help Mom. If anything, I have to become someone great. The fact that I was still breathing meant God had a purpose for me.

The first year of high school went by with ease, with me making straight A's in all my courses. I joined the cross-country team, tried out for the tennis team, and even joined the school choir. Singing gave me a sense of hope. It allowed me to sing my sorrows away. Singing allowed me to connect with my inner self and cry when needed. It gave me relief. Joining after school programs kept me away from the house, but sadly, I still had to go home to do everything. You would think that on the days Auntie Yetunde was not working, she would cook for the house or her parents, but that was not the case. No matter what, both Auntie Yetunde and her mom would wait until I returned from school, only to scold me and say they have been waiting for lunch.

The summer before Sophomore year was challenging for the family. First, Mama moved in with her younger son Segun. Then, we heard Aunt Lola had died. She gave birth to Banji a month before, and shortly after, she died. Aunt Lola and her husband lived in Dublin in Ireland with the rest of their kids. How she died, nobody knows? I overheard the adults saying that the doctor informed them that she died of a brain bleed, but Auntie Yetunde blamed the doctors. She believed they were lying. Even though I hated this family, I couldn't help but feel bad. It was indeed a sad summer. I felt sorry for Grandma and Grandpa. I even felt bad for Auntie Yetunde. Watching her crying and mourning her younger sister saddened my heart. I couldn't help but cry along with her. Aunt Lola was an excellent woman. She didn't deserve to die. Her children—Matthew, Bisi, and the newborn Banji—migrated to America shortly afterwards to live with us. Their father came with them but returned to Dublin after a month. If I thought the house was filled up before, this was another level of crazy. Who needed guests to throw a party when we had all these people?

Summer ended, and fall began. Once again, the school year had started. Tobi and I continued to maintain our secret affair. After cross country practice, he took me to his apartment. Hanging with him was my favorite part, but it was also nerve wracking. I was always worried about getting caught, or Renee accidentally ratting me out to her mom, but she never did. Renee was a great girl, but it was still risky. The hiding and sneaking around sucked the fun out of dating. The first time he took me to his one-bedroom apartment was nice but I didn't like being in there anymore. It was too dirty and messy, and having our first kiss in that room was far from romantic. It sucked. I didn't even know what I was doing. I was resting on his bed when he leaned over to kiss me. His lips touched mine, and he told me that I looked beautiful. I closed my eyes and kissed him back. Honestly, I didn't know what I was supposed to feel. He then stuck his tongue in my mouth, and all it reminded me of was Mr. Michael sticking his tongue in my mouth. As Tobi kissed me, I pulled away. He asked what was wrong, but all I could tell him was for us to stop. Often times, he'd ask me to give him a blow-job, but I would tell him, maybe next time. Since then, hanging out alone in his room made me nervous. I was always afraid something would happen, and the last thing I wanted was sex. We talked about it, but I hoped he would be able to stand us not having sex for a while.

As winter approached, Tobi and I began to grow distant. We hardly saw each other. So, we spent most of our time emailing one another with Yahoo mail. I missed him, and this whole secret relationship was not helping the matter. The only problem was that he had been demanding nudes lately, and it was getting annoying. I didn't like this new Tobi, and I wondered what had come over him. I told him never in my lifetime would I send a naked photo of myself. I would not be one of those stupid high school girls who sent naked pictures of themselves to their boyfriends, only to find them on the internet later. I couldn't risk my reputation. I was too smart for that crap. Besides, him hanging with Teni was not helping the situation.

Teni was another Nigerian girl from church. We both attended the same school and sang in the same choir. She was a senior and two years ahead of me. The good news: she would be graduating soon. She had her eyes on him despite her knowing that we were together. I hated women who go after another woman's man. It just didn't seem right. Honestly, I couldn't blame her alone because they were both at fault. If he wasn't playing along, she wouldn't be flirting with him. Sometimes, all it takes is for the man to set the record straight with these women. The idea of girls fighting one another or women on women fighting all because of a man is stupid.

Watching the two of them in church killed me on the inside. It was worse when Tobi told me he was taking her to prom. This fool pretended to have come to my concert to support me but only to inform me he was taking Teni to prom, which was happening in less than twenty hours. He already had everything ready, which included his tux and car. His hair was well cut, and his beard was groomed too. I wasn't happy, but what could I say? It was the night before the prom. It was too late to object even if I wanted to. He assured me nothing would happen, but a part of me did not believe him.

"This is my first prom. Please? I just want to know what it feels like to go to prom," he said. I looked at him, and I said alright that he could go. Deep down, I was unhappy. Twenty-four hours after their prom, their pictures were all over Facebook. She, in a red silk dress, and him in his red bow tie and red pocket square. Pictures of her kissing him on the cheeks and another picture of her sitting on his lap. I felt disrespected and jealous. When I confronted him, he denied any sort of intimacy. Hearing him say this gave me a sense of relief, but the truth of the matter was I didn't trust him. He had betrayed me.

I continued to ask him, but after a while, I just took his word for it. Deep down, I knew my love and trust for him were never going to be the same again. Giving him my heart was the hardest thing. Sarah and Samantha called me crazy for dealing with his bullsh***. Sarah and Samantha were my friends and the three of us were all in the school choir. Samantha and I were both altos while Sarah sang in a soprano voice. I knew they were right, but I guessed the issue was losing him. I didn't want to lose him. These girls didn't get it. More than anything else, Tobi understood me. He knew all my secrets, my family life, and my birth family. Moreover, we were of the same culture and ethnicity. We spoke the same language. Sarah and Samantha are both Haitians, born and grew up with their family. Sarah and Samantha had no idea about what I was dealing with, and they would never understand even if I told them all that had been happening.

By the end of my sophomore year, I had to drop my after-school programs. Tennis and cross-country practices were not working out. The number of people in the house plus the new baby made things tougher than ever. It was all my responsibility to juggle the care for all the children, the house chores, plus trying to escape Mr. Michael's sexual advances. The first few months after the baby's arrival were cutthroat. I hadn't raised a new child since Raphael was a baby. Every time Banji was up, I also was up. Sleeping was out of the question. I was an excellent runner, but the last thing I wanted was to fail my classes. Sacrificing after-school programs to balance everything else seemed to be worth it. The family ensured my life was a living hell.

Meanwhile, Auntie Yetunde was doing everything to ensure my grades suffered. It seems like this was her new mission after Renee failed her freshman year. She wanted to transfer Renee to a different school to protect her daughter's reputation. The moment we discovered that Renee failed all her courses, Auntie Yetunde and Grandma both blamed me for her failures. Even though Grandma was in Nigeria, she still found ways to cast her blame. She said a lot of hurtful things over the phone that I started to cry. Then, Mr. Michael looked at me and intervened. That night, the commotion stopped, but Grandma never ceased to blame me. She claimed that I enjoyed her granddaughter's failure, and if I'd helped her well enough, she would have passed. The fact was that I had already assisted her in the best way I could which included her homework. I definitely couldn't force her to attend classes or attend the classes on her behalf. In the process of shaming and blaming, we learned that Renee had been skipping some of her classes. No wonder why she failed her exams.

Renee was a nice girl and a social butterfly, which was the basis for skipping classes. She was all about being popular and yes, she was. After the blaming and the shaming, Auntie Yetunde decided to send Renee to a private high school and hid her transcript from the new school despite multiple requests. I don't know how she got away with it, but she did. Over time, the school stopped asking for it. I believed sending her to a private school was good for her. It would give her structure and less freedom. No one needed to tell me to study or go to class before I did so.

Despite the ups and downs, I, on the other hand, was able to finish school and balance home and school life. My GPA dropped due to one B plus, but it was not bad.

At first, I was disappointed in myself because it destroyed my chances of getting scholarships, which was my only way of getting out of the house. But later, I learned that it was okay because it was all on God in the end. I hoped and prayed that God should guide and grant me the opportunity to make it.

In the summer, Grandma and Grandpa came to visit and so, did Aunt Lola's husband. He spent a month and took Banji with him. It was sad to watch him take Banji, but I think it was for the best. I would have preferred that he took Matthew, who was stubborn and always misbehaving. He never listened. He assumed he could do whatever he wanted. Losing his mom didn't give him the right to misbehave and cause trouble. I think, more than anything, he needed a father figure. The absence of his father could lead him down the road of self-destruction. If I could have gotten my wish, I preferred that he took both boys.

CHAPTER FIFTEEN

THIS TOO SHALL PASS

Summer flew by, and I was sure glad that there was no more baby to handle as Grandma and Grandpa went back in Nigeria. Matthew and Bisi were also enrolled in the private school. Everyone started school once again. Renee started her sophomore year at the same private school with the rest of the kids with the exception of Ashley and I, who still attended public schools. Senior year was a home stretch away, then off I went.

The school year continued, and I stayed true to myself, not minding Tobi or his lying self. I started searching for colleges. Each lunchtime and after school, I spent time talking with members of each attending college at different college fairs. One of the days, after school, I met representatives of UMass Lowell. After talking to them, I learned they were offering scholarships with a one-month study program. Without any further questions, I signed up and collected all the necessary information. Going away for a month for medical research was my dream and would be a dream come true. I wanted to experience living on a college campus and being away from home. This was all exciting. The best part about all this was the money. Winning the scholarships and grants would mean a lot to me. The different AP classes I attended had to be useful for something. During the week, I spent time after school writing my essay and submitting the required documents along with my transcript. With my impeccable grades, there was no way I would not be chosen.

After a week, I summoned the courage to tell Auntie Yetunde and Mr. Michael about the university and their scholarship opportunities. Not surprisingly, Auntie Yetunde didn't show much enthusiasm. She just replied, "Okay," with nothing further. Many months passed, and in the middle of March, I got a call from UMass Lowell saying I'd been selected, and I had the opportunity to win their scholarship. Once again, they reiterated the program and scholarship opportunities. I was stunned. It reminded me of the science field trip I was part of in middle school. I was among the ten students selected to work with DNA replication and polymerase. I loved science. This was all coming back as I spoke to their representative. I hung up the house phone in excitement. We had one week to reply to them. A week later, the administrator called back, and unfortunately, I had to decline their offer. Auntie Yetunde never granted her permission. I was bitterly angry, but this only made me more eager to get out of the house. I could have won the scholarship, an opportunity missed within a blink of an eye.

A few weeks after this event, I was in the kitchen prepping dinner when Ashley came to ask me if I was planning on going away. I looked at her in confusion. "What are you talking about?" I asked her.

"When Grandma was here, I heard her and Mommy saying they know you are going to move away once you go to college," she said.

"Oh, don't be silly. I won't," I replied.

"I am really going to miss you if you did," she said.

Deep down in my heart, I felt guilty for lying to her. Ashley was so sweet. Of all the children, she was the only one who tended to check on me. I watched her smile and walked into the living room to join the rest of the kids. I spent the rest of the day thinking about how the parents knew this. For them to be thinking this, they must have a plan to keep me here. Frankly speaking, I didn't think these people wanted me to go to college. I figured that explained why Mr. Michael kept saying, "I'll get you a place of your own instead of having to commute to school."

Thinking about Ashley and the rest of the kids got me feeling bad. I have always been there for them, and they depended on me. It's just that the pressure in the house was too much. I didn't want to be commuting to college. It was sad to say that I didn't know anywhere else apart from school, church, and home. They had enslaved me to the point of not knowing anywhere. I wanted to have friends, go out, and have a normal life. The pressure from this house and Mr. Michael's erotic behavior irritated me. If this continued, I didn't think I was going to last.

I kept thinking about Ashley's statement, but the truth was I didn't know who was better—the husband or the wife. Who could I say I tolerate the most? Both husband and wife were awful. Auntie Yetunde was always insulting my family, and she never allowed us to talk. Mr. Michael, on the other hand, raped me but then treated me nicely afterward. One school night, his wife came home early. The children were asleep upstairs. I was in the kitchen prepping for the next day when he came to grab and drag me to the living room in the basement. He pushed me onto the couch and pulled my shirt down. He started nibbling on my nipple. Not knowing when the wife entered the house, all we heard was the jingle of the keys and footsteps. Mr. Michael, who was getting naked, stopped and quickly pulled up his boxers. He shoved my head to hide me. I had never seen a grown man get so scared. His wife entered the living room, paused for a moment, looking puzzled, and then, she greeted her husband and asked if he was okay. He replied and stated he was just turning off the TV and that he was heading to bed. Together, they walked upstairs to their room. I was shaking the whole time, but part of me wished she would have caught this filthy man she called husband. She deserved to know the truth, the whole truth.

On Saturday, I was upstairs cleaning the room when she came to meet me. She sat on the bed and asked me to have a seat. "I want you to tell me what is going on?" I was so scared.

The palpitation of my heart was a sounding brass. Voice trembling and couldn't speak up. If anything, I knew she saw what happened that night. This goes two ways: for her to take my side, or, for her to support her husband. "I said what is going on between you and my husband?" she said once again. Choking and stuttering on my words, I summoned the courage to tell her. Telling her everything from the beginning was the most difficult thing to do. I started crying and couldn't stop. She placed her left arm on my back and I rested my head on her left shoulder. She seems shocked but not quite upset. She asked me why I didn't tell her, but before I could answer, she replied, "Never mind." She then asked me if I had told anyone, and I said no. "Good," she said.

That was not the reaction I expected. She seems too calm and collected. I wondered what she was thinking. I continued to rest my head on her. After a while, she rubbed my back, got up, and walked away.

Telling her, I felt a great relief. I was so happy and confident that this will be the end of the sexual assaults. As the day went by, it became awkward. The next two weeks in the house were rocky. Nobody was talking to each other. I could tell Auntie Yetunde and her husband were not on talking terms, most especially after their heated argument in the bedroom. The previous week, I was in the children's room when I heard Auntie Yetunde screaming and crying. I figured her husband slapped her. I felt bad for her. When I noticed Mr. Michael left the house, I walked into her room to comfort her. Rubbing her back and wiping away her tears. But after that night, no more arguments.

By the end of the month, everything went back to normal. Auntie Yetunde went back to hanging with her best friends—Yomi and, at times, Nikki. She also went back to shopping, buying clothes, shoes, and jewelry. The kids went back to playing and running around the house. I still had to cook and serve the monster. I couldn't believe everything went back to normal. It just seems like nothing ever happened. Auntie Yetunde went back to her cold ways. Mr. Michael went back to making his sexual advances by slapping and grabbing my butt and boobs. He also went back to finding ways to isolate me in the house or take me to a motel to have his way with me. Every month, I found time to get Auntie Yetunde alone and tell her that her husband was still at it, but she never seemed to care or do anything about it. It was like she had turned a blind eye. After a while, I decided never to report any of the incidences to her. I felt helpless. The person that I felt could do something had suddenly given up, like she became numb to the situation. I couldn't help but think that this too shall pass. Before, it was physical abuse, and that stopped. So, this would stop too.

CHAPTER SIXTEEN

CLARITY IN THE DARKNESS

Although the summer of sophomore year was the worst summer for everyone, good things came out of it for me. Mr. Michael decided to process my papers. My papers mean everything. As he always said, without a green card, I was nothing in this country. I hoped to travel back home and someday reunite with Mom and, hopefully, tell her everything.

Every two years, Mr. Michael traveled home, spent twenty to thirty days, then returned to the States. His traveling was a blessing and a curse. Each time he traveled, I was happy, but the only problem was Auntie Yetunde. I wished both of them could just disappear into thin air. If I must say, Auntie Yetunde was a disappointment to motherhood. I didn't understand how a working-class woman doesn't think she should pay any of the house bills while her husband was away. All she did was shop and buy clothes while the hot water got shut off and other expenses piled up. I had to wake up earlier than usual to boil water so we could all have our baths because the cold weather was unbearable. She was so fully dependent on a man that she couldn't get anything done. But the moment he returned, the bills got paid, and the hot water returned. His return brought about peace and the basic human necessities. And for a moment, I would be happy, but at the same time, devastated.

Since Auntie Yetunde had turned a blind eye to her husband's actions, living in this house has taught me that if I wanted something in life, I had to comply with Mr. Michael's demands even if they were sinful. It was shameful that it had come to this, but my compliance was needed if I planned on seeing my mom again. The truth was, it's not like I complied; I just didn't bother struggling during the process. When I struggled, I only ended up getting injured by either scraping my arms or legs or banging my body on foreign objects. My injuries depended on the location. The other thing was him getting physically aggressive with me, and I didn't want that. Whenever he wanted it, I've learned it was best to lay down. I would sometimes cry but didn't fight it. When he finished, I'd put my clothes on, wipe my tears, and walk away.

The good news was that he was a man of his word. Since I'd been cooperative with his demands, he fulfilled his promise. As he had promised, he worked on my travel documents while my green card was in process. In April of 2012, he decided to grant me my wish to travel back home to visit mom. Ashley wanted to travel along, and I was glad it would not be him and me alone. Flying by Delta Air Lines, we landed in Lagos, Nigeria. It had been a while since I went home, and I was excited to meet everyone. In the first week and a half, we stayed at Ashley's cousin's hotel in Lagos. By the end of the second week, we headed to Akure. In the car was Mr. Michael, his friend who was also the driver, Ashley, and I. It was a long six-hour drive. I'd been gone for so long that I had forgotten how Nigerian roads and communities looked. Everything looked different. We arrived at Grandma's house in Oke-aro, where Ashley and I would be staying. We learned that Grandma and Grandpa had traveled, and Grandma had ordered us to stay at her house. She ordered Timothy, the next-door neighbor, to look after us. I didn't care where she and her husband had gone to. In fact, I was happy she was not home.

We got to Akure so late in the evening. Mr. Michael and his friend dropped us off and headed to the nearest motel to check in. Standing outside and waiting for our arrival was Timothy. He was six feet two inches in height, slender looking, with fair skin complexion, and handsome. It had been a while since I'd been back home, and by the way he shouted my name, I could tell he remembered me even though I couldn't say the same about him. Grandma always talked about him and on a few occasions, I had witnessed her talking to him on the phone. She loved Timothy, and if she could pick a man for me, it would be him. Also, Timothy has reached out to me on Facebook messenger a couple of times, but I ignored him. Seeing him in person was different. He was very handsome. The idea of Grandma hooking us up was never going to happen. I don't trust her and the fact that I knew his family and Mrs. Babalola were close friends made me not trust them or him even more. But still, after all these years, I could not believe they were still living here. I looked at him once more and then looked at Ashley who ran to hug him. He helped carry our belongings and we walked up the stairs and into the house.

I looked around the house and surprisingly, the house still looked very much the same after all these years, with the same old color. The well in the atrium was still the same, and so was the firewood used for cooking. Everything looked very much as it was with the exception that I was much taller and older making the surroundings somehow smaller. Everything didn't seem as huge as it was. The old tenants were gone except Timothy's mom. The atrium located in the back was still as it was.

As we entered the house, we took a seat on one of the couches. He greeted us once more and hugged Ashley while wrapping his arm around her waist. It was a long night with no electricity. As it got darker in the room, Timothy lit the candles and lanterns. We sat and talked all evening. Timothy said Grandma always talked about me. And by the expression and smile on his face, I could tell he liked me. I wondered what Grandma had said to him. We stared at each other, but I never asked what was said. Around 10:00 to 11:00 P.M., we made our bed and prepped for sleep. Timothy said his goodbye on his way downstairs. He reported that he would be back in the morning.

The next morning, he made us breakfast of boiled yams and fried eggs. After breakfast, late in the early morning, Mr. Michael and his friend showed up at the house. Ashley had planned to follow me to Ilara, but somehow, her dad had convinced her to stay back with Timothy while he and I drive to Ilara to visit my mom. I hated this idea and I hated being alone with him. He was the type of man that would steal every chance to satisfy his sexual urges. He told me to hurry along to let us go. Ashley and Timothy followed us downstairs to say goodbye. In the white Lexus was his blossoms friend. He opened the car door and told me to get in, I turned around to look at Ashley and Timothy, and deep down, I knew what was about to happen. But then again, I thought maybe I was wrong. How could he possibly have his way? We are in Nigeria! Also, his friend is here with us. No way would he do such a thing in front of his friend, and risk being exposed. These were my thoughts as I sat in the car quietly. Yet, again, why wasn't I convinced? Why do I feel like he would? I started to cry on the inside. I couldn't believe this was happening in Nigeria too. I have the choice to make because this man has the power——the power to control if I get to visit my mom. I got inside the car and closed the door. As I thought, instead of heading straight to Ilara, we took a turn and headed to a motel. The area was quiet, with few scattered trees. I looked around, and there was nobody. "What are we doing here?" I asked.

"Auntie Dami, I just need to grab something that I forgot in my room. Let's go inside," he said.

"I prefer to wait here," I replied.

He and his friend got out of the car and went inside the room. I waited for a while, but there were no signs of them coming out. So, I took a seat by their doorstep as the car was getting too hot and unbearable by the heat. Later, his friend came out. I watched him get inside his car and drive off. I turned around to peep inside and noticed Ashley's dad lying in bed, enjoying his fresh air conditioner while watching TV.

"Don't be stubborn, Auntie Dami. I thought you want to see your mom," he said. Before I could do anything, he rose, rushed towards me, grabbed, and pulled me inside. I screamed because I thought I would fall, but he covered my mouth and locked his door.

"Please! Please don't do this," I begged. I continued to plead, but it was to no avail. He whipped out his penis and inserted it in me. Struggling underneath him, all I could hear was him grunting and moaning. I continued to struggle and shoved him, but he twisted and pinned my arms over my head, his sweat dripping on me. Then, when he finished, he fell on his back and fell asleep. I laid there for a moment, watching him snore. The thought of smothering him with the pillow came across my mind. Part of me wanted to choke him in his sleep, but the words of the Bible came across my mind. "Thou shall not kill." I can't do this. Killing him wouldn't make me see my mom. I began to sob, then went into his bathroom to wash my female area.

The sound of the running water woke him up. "You ready? Let's go. I'll call my friend to find out where he's at," he said.

Sitting on one of the chairs, I pretend not to hear him. I sat there thinking, *Did this devil's son just ejaculate inside of me?* I prayed that I was not pregnant. This man was an animal! This man was a monster! He would never do this to his daughters, but instead, he did that to me. This was the man I called Daddy in front of everyone. This was a man that is supposed to be my protector, but instead, he found every way to get me alone and satisfy his sexual pleasures. I looked at him and placed a curse upon him that it would never be well with him. I swore to myself that this will be his last day and that he would never get his way ever again. I owed it to myself.

"Auntie Dami," he called.

I looked up at him, and for the first time, I said, "You are sick! God will punish you."

He looked at me in disbelief then chuckled. He then answered, "You are so stubborn. So, you'll prefer to give it to the small boys out there. Those little boys that can't do anything for you. Small boys like Tobi. All they will do is sleep with you for free and then dump you after. Look at all the things I am doing for you. You should be cooperating so I can help your mom."

He opened the door, and his friend was outside in the car, parked and waiting for us. Mr. Michael walked out, and I followed behind. We got inside, and we made a turn to Grandma's house. For a moment, I thought we were not going to Ilara anymore because I had upset him, but instead, when we got to the house, he called out to Ashley to join us to go to the village. She came down and got in the car. "Daddy, I thought you guys went to see Auntie Dami's mom," said Ashley.

"Yes! We turned around and figured we should all go together," he replied. Timothy came down after and entered the car too. I glanced at Ashley and said nothing.

It was a quiet ride to Ilara. I was angry but sad. I couldn't stop thinking about home. It had been ages since I last saw my mom. We got to the Ilara junction and made a turn toward my village. My heart pounded, I was full of mixed emotions, not knowing whether I should be happy about seeing my mom or upset about what had just happened a few hours ago.

We arrived at the red gate that looked like it was about to fall apart. The gate door squeaked as I pushed it open. This gate looked like it was hanging on by a thread. The house looked smaller than how I used to picture it, the walls dirty and stained. I turned my head to look at the pavement where my dad was buried, but Mom came running out before I could finish. She went to the floor and began rolling and kissing the filthy dusty pavement. Her happiness was over the moon. She prayed and continued to thank God for journey mercy. I watched her as she continued to roll on the floor. My eyes didn't actually leave her when she got up and led us to the living room. She served us rice and stew. I sat there, staring at my plate of food. I didn't have the appetite to eat, but I managed to take a few bites. She looked at me and asked if I was okay while touching my face and holding my hands. "Are you sick?" she asked and then felt my forehead. I shook my head and said no in Yoruba. I looked at her and all I see was her incoming gray hair and her rough wrinkly face. *Man… Mom is old,* I thought to myself. Her once youthful skin had become old and wrinkly. I could tell she was suffering. I felt tears in my eyes. I wanted to cry but couldn't. I was holding my tears back. She held me once again and I smiled at her. A part of me wanted to pull her to one corner to tell everything, but I couldn't.

Not now, I told myself. It is too soon to break the bad news.

When everyone was done, we spent about another thirty minutes together, and then planned to head back. Mom continued to thank Mr. Michael. Mr. Michael offered Mom to come to Akure with us, but she refused and said maybe later in the week. As we were about to leave, Bisola and Debby, the two youngest of my sisters, returned from school. I barely remembered them or knew who was who. They greeted us and Mom introduced me to them as their older sister, even though, I could tell they knew. They went inside to change out of their school uniforms. When asked, Mom said they could come the next day to spend time with us in Akure. I looked at Timothy, and I was surprised that he knew my siblings and Mom more than anything else. When I tried making conversation with them, Mom, Debby, and Bisola just looked at me like I had three eyes. None of them were understanding me. I knew I was speaking Yoruba. I guessed my accent had changed. That is what living in America does. Mom kept staring, smiling, and touching and feeling my skin. I could tell she was thrilled.

We headed back to Akure, and two days later, Auntie Yetunde called us on the phone and started yelling that I shouldn't be going to my mom's place. Her exact words: "It is not every day you'll be going there. Do you understand?" It's ridiculous that I only spent about one and half hours with my mom since we landed and she was on the phone talking nonsense. To avoid trouble, Ashley and I spent the rest of the second week and some parts of the third week in Akure at Grandma's house. Meanwhile, Mr. Michael continued to stay at his motel. Bisola and Debby came to visit and stay with us. They spent a few days and then headed back to Ilara. Afterward, Tiwa, my other sister, came to spend a night. The first night together, Mr. Michael and his driver friend took Ashley, Tiwa, and me out to the bar. A waiter came over, and Mr. Michael ordered fish and chips while trying to get Tiwa and me to drink his alcohol.

The good thing about my family was that we don't drink. Alcohol was considered wrong and should not be ingested by a child of God. Although Ashley was young, he allowed her to order Smirnoff ice that contained five percent alcohol. We sat there at the round table, waiting for our orders when I noticed Mr. Michael and his friend staring at Tiwa. He whispered in my ears to tell me how sexy my sister looked and how his friend was interested. "Look at those boobs," he said.

I was infuriated on the inside but kept my cool. Instead, I told Tiwa to stay close to me. I watched Mr. Michael's friend trying to make moves on her. Watching these men whisper to each other and stare at my sister made me nervous and scared about what might happen next. I pulled Tiwa closer. Throughout the night, I monitored her closely until they took us back home. I was glad the night was over and that nothing happened to any of us.

The next day, Tiwa and I spent the afternoon together, and then she returned to Ilara. Sister Ade showed up a few hours later, then off she went too. The next day, Ashley and I got our hair braided. On my last day in Akure, Mom came to visit. She held me and told me to be good and that Mr. Michael had been telling her that I am stubborn. I attempted to tell her what has been happening, but the moment I opened my mouth to talk, she hushed me and then continued to express how Grandma had been scolding and blaming her for my misbehavior. She said Grandma accused her of my attitude. Both Mom and I knew that these statements weren't true. That wicked family never let us talk. They did everything to keep us apart. So, how was it possible that she was corrupting me? Listening to Mom, I could tell that she was not going to listen to what I was about to tell her. They corrupted her mind because she didn't bother questioning their ways or the lies they had told her.

Standing and listening to the words coming out of her mouth, I realized she was rendered so helpless, and for a long time, I stayed with these people because of her. Her words reminisced in my mind, and I promised myself never to run away because I knew nothing lasts forever. The reality was that Grandma had no respect for anybody, and Ashley's dad was only moved by sex.

Grandma had always treated Mom poorly. Her fragile self, however, never stood her ground but instead, tolerated Grandma's insults. Even after everything, she would go ahead to apologize to them because she wanted peace. Mom was always afraid of what society would think. She feared public opinion and preferred to keep everything on the down-low. I hated this character of hers, but at the same time, I understood. Nigerian society is rough. Everybody would prefer to keep things on the down-low on any given day instead of speaking out. The level of social pressure can make one commit suicide. I wanted to make her proud by not running away. The old me would have run away, but because I was in a new world with new people, running away didn't seem plausible. Moreover, I didn't know where to run to in this situation.

So, she scolded me for exposing my body. "Your body belongs to God." "Did you hear me?" she stated. She told me to stop being stubborn because she knew I got that behavior from my dad. "Your dad was a stubborn man." She also informed me that the only person we have in this world is God. Lastly, she told me to be good. "Be good, do everything they tell you."

In the end, all I could say was, "okay". She then left back to Ilara. The next day, Mom showed up early in the morning before we headed back to Lagos. It was a hard goodbye. I cried. Then, we headed off. We made it to Lagos by evening and checked into the same hotel once more. For the next two days, Ashley and I hung around with her cousins. Grandma and Grandpa came to join us at the hotel on our last day. Uncle Ojo also showed up. He helped us pack, and then we headed to the airport.

The journey back to the States was depressing. Sitting on the airplane, landing at Boston airport, and getting home, I couldn't help but think of how disappointing the trip was. All I ever wanted was to stay back with my family. I cannot believe I am back in this country. The worst part was that Mom and I never got a chance to spend quality time together. Now, I am back in the States without her knowing my truth: the truth about Auntie Yetunde and her husband. The truth of how they have changed my identity, or how Aunt Miriam almost adopted me and kept me as her child.

Maybe, this was Auntie Yetunde and Grandma's plan. That must have been the reason they kept calling to yell at me to stay put in Grandma's house. This must be their plan, to keep me away, and prevent me front telling Mom the truth. The night after we went to the bar with Tiwa, I learned that Auntie Yetunde enrolled me in school because of the social pressure in Akure. Evidently, news had spread across the towns in Oke-aro that Auntie Yetunde and her mother were using me as a housemaid in addition to selling me to other families to make money. To think about it, this explained why they came to remove me from Aunt Mariam's house.

The whole ride back to Massachusetts, I kept thinking Tiwa was right because it didn't make sense for a family that didn't want me to suddenly start fighting to keep me. I couldn't help thinking the fight that broke out between the two friends was because of money. The fastest way to end a friendship was through money. Aunt Mariam had started my adoption papers, and Auntie Yetunde and Grandma didn't like the idea. The adoption would terminate the operation of their money-making machine. No wonder she sends me to her distant friend in the Boston area to help her cook and clean for Nigerian parties. I thought I was really making money, not knowing it was part of her plan to exploit me for money. In the end, the lady would pay me, but only for Auntie Yetunde to make me share the money with her girls as if they were slaving in the kitchen along with me. In the end, she would borrow the rest of the money in my hand, pretending she would pay it back. I was so naïve. It is not really borrowing if you never pay the person back their money.

I lay in bed throughout the night, thinking about how these people got their way. Their plan worked. I didn't even get the chance to tell Mom my truths. But again, I was upset with her, she just hushed me and told me to be good, not caring what I had to say. I hated the fact that Nigerian parents never listen to their children. As I lay in bed, tears started pouring down my face. I told myself that I have to be strong because it was the only way to survive. Everything was for a short period. School would be starting soon and one more year of high school and then college. If these people think they could prevent me from going to college, then they have another thing coming.

My return from Nigeria opened my eyes. For some reason, after my last tears shed in bed that night, I felt stronger in spirit. I felt like nothing could get me down, not even Tobi and Teni's relationship. I noticed how my trip had given them a reason to be closer, closer than before. The Sunday after we returned, we went to a church barbecue. Sitting at my table were Auntie Yetunde and her church friends. I sat at their table quietly, watching other children play. At the barbecue were also Teni and Tobi. Auntie Yetunde noticed the two sitting together and laughing. Everyone at the barbecue was talking about their relationship. "I told you so. Do you see that? See your life? That's the Tobi you were lusting over. That is him with Teni," she whispered in my ear. She continued to remind me of the incident as we were driving home. I never said anything. The girls looked at me and stayed quiet. Every youth in church talked about their relationship. When I finally got the chance to ask Tobi, he denied it once again. He said they were just friends. Even though he said this, my gut knew that I shouldn't trust him. It was obvious that they were both into each other that even a blind person could tell. Knowing me, Tobi understood that I didn't trust him. So, he did everything to gain his love once again. He messaged me and sent an email. For a while, he stopped asking for nudes. He even came to visit me after school. No matter how much he tried, all I remembered was the betrayal. After a while of trying, I accepted his friendship. We agreed to be friends for the time being until I feel like I could trust him again. Although he agreed, Tobi never stopped pursuing the love we once shared. The secret cell phone Uncle Amos once got me was exposed when Auntie Yetunde went through my backpack while I was sleeping. Her discovery of my secret phone rattled me for a while, but I learned to accept it. Maybe, Tobi and I weren't meant to be together.

At first, Auntie Yetunde screamed and yelled but later returned the phone to me. She told me that I could use it. I guess she didn't find anything disturbing. I was smart enough to delete my conversations with him, most especially of him asking for nudes.

CHAPTER SEVENTEEN

FINDING STRENGTH

June approached, and just as I suspected, I didn't see my period. I knew I was pregnant by my late cycle. I told Mr. Michael, but he didn't believe me. We took two home pregnancy tests, which the results turned out negative. One month and two weeks passed, and still no period. I started to get lightheaded around the house, but no nausea or vomiting. I woke up every morning, starving.

Towards the end of the month, he asked if I saw my period, but I said no. When he came to terms with the incident, he couldn't help but keep asking if I had slept with Timothy. I looked at him and said nothing. But then, he started panicking. "We have to get rid of this Auntie Dami. You are only in high school, and you can't be pregnant." he said. "Think about it, what do you think the church will say with you carrying a big belly everywhere? No, no, no!" he continued. Without giving it a second thought, he punched my stomach. I gasped my stomach in pain and agony. My eyes were wide in surprise as I stared at him, wondering what had just happened. He ordered me to lay on the bed and so I did. I plead for him to stop because this wasn't working. "Auntie Dami, don't you get it? You can't be pregnant!" He continued. As I lay there, he sat on my stomach, got up, and used his fist to press on my stomach in a downward motion. I grunted and the pain surged through my body in a torrent. He assumed doing that would get rid of the growing fetus. The next day he asked if my period started and I said no. The following day he asked again, and I said nothing.

After all his wasted efforts, he took me to a private doctor to get properly tested. According to the doctor, this time, the result came back positive, and I was eight weeks pregnant. Now that the doctor confirmed that I was pregnant, being devastated was an understatement. I sat in the doctor's office and, like always, was numb with no signs of emotion, not even anger. I sat in the hospital chair with my mind hazed, thousands of thoughts crossing my mind. *This man has killed me.* The ride home felt like an eternity. I cried in bed every day. I thought I was done for good and my plans out the window.

"Listen, on Thursday, we are going somewhere. Okay?" Mr. Michael told me a few days later. Thursday arrived, Mama came to stay with the kids, Auntie Yetunde went to work, and Mr. Michael and I went to the doctor. The ride was not an ordinary ride to Boston, especially with being blindfolded and being told to lay flat on the passenger seat. I wondered why he had to blindfold me. Stopping at the parking lot, he coached me on what to say to the doctor. We headed inside the big building. I was scared, but I knew that I must be brave. I wiped my tears but continued to follow him. "You know, you should be lucky and happy that I am doing this for you. Besides, I cannot risk your mommy finding out or for you to start throwing up," he said. "Just follow what I say. Do you hear me?" He added. I nodded my head, and we entered via a double door, and took the elevator that led us upstairs to the doctor's office located to the left. We walked inside, opened the door, and took our seats. There were two young people in the waiting room, sitting and waiting patiently. The lady to our right was surely pregnant. In one hand was her phone. Mr. Michael walked up to the receptionist and after a few conversations, the receptionist handed him a piece of paper. He grabbed the paper and handed it over to me to fill out the forms. Filling the form out, he leaned over my shoulder and watched. I filled out the information, signed the form, and handed it back to him, which he then took back to the receptionist.

Mr. Michael returned to his seat and waited for us to get called in. When it was time, a nurse stood by the doorway and called my name; I wasn't shocked by her wrong pronunciation. Most Americans have that tendency. I got up and went inside. Mr. Michael attempted to get up when the lady nurses signaled with hand gestures. I watched him relax back into his seat. "She will be back shortly," the lady said. The nurse led me straight into the bathroom and handed me a urine cup and a cleansing wipe. I followed the instructions as directed and when I finished, I returned to the waiting room.

Later, the nurse asked me to come back inside. At the sound of, "The doctor will", Mr. Michael jumped out of his seat. He looked at me and I stared back at him. I walked into the doctor's office and Mr. Michael followed behind. "Please have a seat," the doctor said and before anything else, Mr. Michael grabbed the next seat. The doctor introduced himself. "Before we begin, is it okay for this man to be here?" The doctor asked. Before I could answer, Mr. Michael tugged on my trouser. I nodded and then answered yes to his question. Many questions were asked: "Who is this person sitting next to you? How did you get pregnant, and, are you sure you want to do this?" Each question was answered as rehearsed. It crossed my mind to tell the doctor the truth and expose the devil for his evil deed. The man I called "father," was a monster, a rapist, and the one who was responsible for my pregnancy. Unfortunately, that was not what came out of my mouth. The question of "If I was sure if I wanted to do this" was asked multiple times, and each time the doctor asked, the monster pulled on my trouser. All I could do was nod and say "yes" each time he asked.

After a while, the doctor wrapped up the questioning and gave me two pills. "Take this now with water. This pill stops the fetus from growing. It stops the hormone. On Saturday, place the other pill in your cheek and let it dissolve. This will wash it out... Okay?" he explained. "In four weeks, come back to get a checkup just to be sure the pills work. Okay?" he added.

Mr. Michael thanked the doctor, and we headed out. I turned around to take a last look at the doctor, then went out the door. The doctor glanced back then went back to writing something on the paper on his desk. He seemed disappointed by the look on his face. I was disappointed in myself too. I was disappointed in not being able to speak up despite being asked several times. That was my golden opportunity, but again, fear took over because I was thinking of Mom. It was the fear of not knowing what will happen if I told the truth. It was a fear for my safety and my mom's safety.

It was a long drive home. Anything the monster had to say during the entire ride was all a haze. When we got to the parking lot, he took out the pill from the paper box, crushed the empty box, and hid it inside his car. He then put the tiny pill in his pocket and walked inside the house.

I went inside to continue the remaining house chores. On Saturday morning, I woke up and went downstairs to make breakfast for the house. Everyone was home, including Auntie Yetunde, who was sitting in the living room watching TV and talking with Auntie Yomi on the phone.

Mr. Michael walked up to me in the kitchen and handed me the pill. I opened up the tiny sachet and placed the pill on my cheek and left it to dissolve as directed by the doctor. Mr. Michael then grabbed the sachet and placed it in his pocket. Not long after, I felt a gush of fluid rushing out. I rushed out of the kitchen and ran to the upstairs bathroom to check what had happened. Looking into my underwear, I noticed a translucent jelly-like substance in my underwear followed by a gush of blood. Sitting on the toilet, I grabbed some tissues and began poking at them. Then, I felt another gush of blood. It was excruciating with severe cramps and bleeding. Nobody says the pain will be this much. I managed to clean up and then head straight to Auntie Yetunde's room to take some pads. After, I went back downstairs to finish cooking, served breakfast, and began the house cleaning.

At the four-week mark, we returned to the hospital for re-evaluation. The doctor confirmed that I was still pregnant. I looked at Mr. Michael, and he looked disappointed. "You need to come back in another four weeks. If you are still pregnant, then we might need to do surgery, but I don't think you will need it because you are still very much bleeding," the doctor said. Another four weeks passed, and we went back to the doctor. Even though I was still actively bleeding, this time, the doctor confirmed that I was no longer pregnant. Mr. Michael excitedly thanked the doctor, and we headed out. I could sense the high relief in his voice. He was so excited that he started blasting the radio on our way home. I sat in the car quietly. I knew that I should be happy that it was over, but I was not.

How could I be happy? My life was a convoluted mess—once pregnant, but it was now aborted. I have sinned against God, and I hoped that He had mercy upon me. For weeks, I felt lost, numbed, and not able to communicate with God. I watched everyone go about their normal lives, especially Mr. Michael. One night, I got on my knees, prayed, and cried to God. As I prayed, I felt a sense of relief. God was a merciful God. I didn't feel any shame or guilt for the life I lost. Also, I didn't blame myself, but once in a while, I would subconsciously cry.

September came, and once again, the school started again. It had been three months, and still, I was bleeding. After three months of physical pain in my lower abdomen, my uterine wall contracting and shredding apart, and finally, the pain decreased as each day passed. The worst part was watching this monster walk around the house, humming, and going about his daily life like nothing ever happened. *Is it normal to bleed for this long?* I thought. I wished I had someone to ask this question. The sharp pain and the bleeding stopped in the middle of September, which was three and a half months later. I had never been happier. I was happy that my body had gone back to normal.

In the same month of September, a week after I had stopped bleeding, another event occurred. It was Friday, and I was in the bathroom in my bath towel, brushing my teeth and getting ready for school when I noticed the doorknob shaking as if someone were trying to open it. I was stunned.

The kids were already downstairs, waiting for their father to drop them at school. I turned my head only to see Mr. Michael unlocking the door. He peeped, and when he realized it was me, he walked in and closed the door. He walked up to me and then slapped and grabbed my butt while whispering, "I noticed you are no longer bleeding…umm, Auntie Dami." Hearing his voice irritated me. I was angry, and I lost it. I shrugged my left shoulder, causing my elbow to hit him. He pulled away and let my butt go. I watched him walk away with a smirk on his face. I was angry. Staring at my reflection in the mirror, I knew I had it. This was the last straw. I was fed up with this family. I needed to leave this house, and I didn't care what was going to happen. I was exhausted, exhausted from sleeping with one eye open, tired of sleeping with trousers and belts, bundling up like I am going to war. I was tired of listening to mom's voice telling me to be good and tired of being scared.

Standing alone in the bathroom, I realized that this monster would not stop. He would never stop. Staring at my reflection, I realized that I was becoming a shadow of myself and that I needed to be happy. At that moment, I realized that I had to run away. It was the only way. It was either I died in this house or died outside trying to survive. There and at that moment, I made up my mind. I finished getting ready and walked to school.

That day, school was a mess. I didn't learn anything. Playing repeatedly in my head was him grabbing my ass. It was unbelievable that a week after I stopped bleeding, he had started making advances. With the school day being a cloud of a distant memory, I was sure glad the sixth period was a free class period. I went to the library to work on my homework and to write my farewell letter to Auntie Yetunde. I took a seat by the computer and Jane, my classmate, came to sit next to me.

Jane, a Black American girl, was five feet, six inches tall. Her hair was always in a ponytail, and she always wore scarves. Jane was intelligent and artistic. I admired that about her. Since we only had history classes together, we didn't see each other much. I would love to be her friend. She was different from Samantha and Sarah. I loved the way she carried herself. Her appearance seemed responsible, unlike most teenage girls, who only worried about boys and sleep around. By her demeanor, I could tell she was not like them. "Can I sit here?" she asked. "Hi, and of course," I said to her. She replied and greeted back. She took a seat.

I didn't know when I started blabbing about my life's drama, but I didn't care. She was attentive and listened to every word. Although I didn't go into details or tell her exactly the problem, I looked at her, and I knew that she understood me. But again, this is America. By now, I have learned that all a child has to say is 'they don't feel safe,' and that would be it for the family. The state would take over. Auntie Yetunde had warned me in the past that if I ever reported, the state would take me away and I would never see my family again. This statement scared me. The state taking me away was the last thing I wanted. I wanted to see my family and protect my mom. Most importantly, I wanted to go back to Nigeria. After I finished blabbing, she told me about an adjustment counselor named Mrs. Velez.

"You should talk to her, and she is very good at helping students in difficult situations," she said.

"Okay," I replied.

Hmm, Mrs. Velez, I thought. I thanked her, and we ended the day. She went her way, and I did the same.

Being an introvert, I had learned to read people. I am the type of person who sits in one corner and studies people from the outside. One thing my experience has taught me is how to be a good judge of character. So deep down, I knew Jane was a good person at heart.

Aside from Tobi, she was the first person I ever opened up to. Talking with her, I knew she could be trusted. I knew she wouldn't tell anyone unless I wanted her to. Also, opening up to her made me feel better. I left the library and went home immediately to start my chores. Walking home, I made a call to Tobi to tell him about my plan of running away. He was shocked. He kept on asking if I was sure and where do I plan to go or stay? I told him, "I don't know, but I have made up my mind". In reality, I wasn't sure of where to stay, but continuing to live with Auntie Yetunde and her husband would get me killed.

As planned, once I got home, I was determined in packing. I started my chores and later that night, I began packing my clothes alongside some shoes. I hid the bag within the messy stockpiled clothes closet. The next night, I continued to pack my clothes, adding to the ones already folded into the large brown duffel bag. On Sunday evening, I went into Renee's parents' room. The best part about being the housemaid is I know where everything is kept and everyone's schedule. Mr. Michael had gone out, and Auntie Yetunde was at work.

In their room, underneath the TV and behind the table, was a hidden combination-lock suitcase. I took it out, entered the pin, and unlocked the suitcase that contained everyone's legal documents. I searched through piles of papers, gathering every legal document that belonged to me. If it had my name on it, I took it. After collecting everything, I locked the suitcase and hid it where it was kept. I took the papers to the children's room and placed them underneath the mattress to prevent Auntie Yetunde from spotting them. I knew she always went through my backpack. So, my backpack was not an option. For the next few days, I spent time going back and forth, ensuring all necessary documents, including school papers and health records, were obtained.

On Monday, in history class, Jane and I continued from where we left off in the library. "I'll take you to Mrs. Velez right after school to introduce you. She is my auntie," she uttered. Even though I was nervous, all I could say was "okay" to her. I was the type of person that didn't show my emotion, no matter the circumstances. As planned, after school, we went to the yellow building basement to meet Mrs. Velez in her office. But seriously, this part of the school was creepy. As we walked closer, I noticed the opposite side of the basement was the classroom for the wood workshop. I'd been there during my sophomore year for my elective class, but I hadn't been here after that. I was surprised that the teachers' office could be located in such a place—no wonder most students didn't come to this side of the building.

We entered a huge yellow-painted room. On one side was a secretary desk and along the side was a grey cubicle. We approached the cubicle and knocked on the wall. Sitting inside and facing her computer was Mrs. Velez, a Spanish woman with long jet-black hair and greys streaks. Hair tied in a ponytail. Jane introduced me, and then she left. "Hi, I am Mrs. Velez, but you can call me Helen," she said. "Come inside and take a seat," she continued.

I took a seat and then she asked me to tell her what was going on. Not know where to start or what to say, so I just stared at the floor. "My birth mom lives in Nigeria, and my adopted family are not treating me…they are…" I started to cry, and she offered me a tissue. "The family I lived with have been…" she interrupted me and then asked if I have a job? I said no. "How do you like to help me with the after-school program down here? You will be helping some of your peers in tutoring. Are you interested?" I answered yes, and then she took me to her tutoring room to show me around. She went back to her cubicle and on her computer, pulled up my transcript, and checked my grades. I could tell that she was impressed. "Straight A's. Mrs. Anderson is your guidance counselor in the red building," she muttered. "Yes," I replied. "Alright, no problem," she said. Mrs. Anderson was my academic counselor, but I never had an academic problem, so I don't see her much or deal with her. I thanked her, then left and returned home.

I was leaving this house no matter what. I lay in bed on Monday night, wondering what day will be the perfect day to move out without anyone seeing me. On Tuesday, I returned to Helen's office, and as planned, I helped her set up the tutoring room and prep for the tutoring section. A few kids came in for math and science assistance. Helen went back into her cubicle. Once in a while, she would pop her head in to see how things were going.

After work, we discussed my move. "Tomorrow after work, we go pick your things, okay?" She said. "Alright," I answered.

Wednesday was a perfect day: the kids' mother didn't get home until after 7 P.M. and their father wouldn't get to the house until around 5:00 to 5:30 P.M. This would give me the chance to get my stuff. The children would be home, but I didn't think it mattered at this point. Tuesday night was the nerve-racking night of my life. I placed a phone call to Tobi and let him know that I was leaving the next day. He asked if I was ready, and I said yes and that I was done packing a few of my clothes. Tomorrow would be very quick; I'd pick up my duffle bag and drop the letter I had written onto Auntie Yetunde's pillow. Tobi said nothing but "alright."

I later called Ashley into the room and let her know that I was leaving. Renee already knew about my move, so I figured I would also let Ashley know. I promised her that once in a while I would be reaching out to check how she was doing. She looked at me and hugged me. "I am going to miss you, Auntie Dami," she said. I looked at her and hugged her back. She smiled and went to bed. By looking into her eyes, I know she was sad to see me go. Ashley had matured. She had become the type of person who showed concern for others. Renee, on the other hand, was a character of her own. She was just in her little world. Of all the children, I was going to miss Ashley the most. Deep down, I knew it would be hard to keep my promise because it doesn't make sense to be running away from a family but at the same time, trying to keep in touch with them. It just defeats the purpose of running away.

Wednesday came, and it was like every other day. I grabbed the documents underneath the kids' mattress and placed them in my backpack. Then I went to school. I went about my daily routines, including classes, and after-school tutoring. Getting close to the time, my heart started to rise. I couldn't help but hurry Helen. I looked at the time, and it was almost 4:30 P.M. If we didn't start leaving, I might as well kiss running away goodbye. Mr. Michael usually got home around five to five-thirty. By the time we were done, it was 4:35, we closed the classroom and started heading to the house. I couldn't help but start panicking. If we were lucky, we might not get caught. The good news was the house was only a ten minutes' drive. I sat in the car, praying we made it before Mr. Michael got to the house. We arrived at the house by 4:50, and I noticed the monster's car was not home. I felt relieved, but he would be here at any moment from now.

Helen pulled up to the parking lot, and before she could put the car to park, I hopped out and ran inside the house. Raphael and Bisi were downstairs in the small living room while Demola and Matthew are outside in the backyard playing. I ran upstairs, grabbed the brown duffle bag and the other cloth-like green suitcase that were in the hidden clothes closet, and then dropped the letter on the children's parents' bed.

I was on my last two staircases when I saw a large brown foot about to climb the stairs. I looked up, and there he was. In his white lab coat, Mr. Michael and his black work bag carried across his right shoulder. My heart sunk. I knew he would be home by this time. He grabbed my right wrist and pulled me. Right behind him was Helen. I was surprised to see her inside.

"Where are you going, Auntie Dami, and who is this woman?" he shouted.

"LET HER GO!" Helen shouted.

Helen grabbed my duffle bag to assist me. We managed to make our way through the tiny hallway and into the open kitchen. Mr. Michael continued to drag me by my shirt.

"LET HER GO NOW!" Helen shouted once again. The three of us continued to struggle from the kitchen and into the children's living room. Mr. Michael latched on to my wrist for a better hold. Finally, we made it outside. As we got outside, Helen grabbed my other wrist. The kids all gathered, watching, and making so much noise.

"LET HER GO NOW BEFORE I CALL THE PO-LICE!" Helen shouted. At the mention of the name, *police*, he let go of my wrist. I stormed off after Helen. We entered the car and fastened our seatbelts. The moment I was able to catch my breath, I looked up, and there he was, the monster, standing and looking as we pulled out of the driveway.

TO BE CONTINUED…

GLOSSARY

1. **Akure** is the capital of Ondo State, a city in south-west Nigeria.

2. **Well** - underground water created by digging and drilling the ground to create water access. Due to the lack of running water in most African homes, wells are built in the compound to grant people access to water.

3. **Bride price** - Western Nigerian tradition of the groom's family buying requested items by the bride's family. The list of demanded items consists of many foods, clothing materials, and large sums of money.

4. **Ankara** - an African fabric made of multiple unique colors.

5. **Garri** - Western African dish which is made of processed cassava.

6. **Elubo** - yam flour; yam cut into small pieces, fried, and then grounded into smooth brown flour.

7. **Yoruba** - one of many spoken languages in Nigeria.

8. **Gele** - Nigerian head tie/wrap

9. **Sachet water** - cleaned water sold in a plastic bag

10. **Iru** - locust beans; condiments

11. **Efo-riro** - local Nigerian soup made of green leafy vegetables; it's similar to spinach. Efo-riro also contains many assorted lumps of meat and spices.

12. **Egusi soup** - soup made of blended melon seeds and green leafy vegetables.

13. **Jollof rice** - Nigerian rice dish- usually orange in color. It's cooked with blended tomatoes, red bell peppers, onion, thyme, habanero pepper for spices, and many seasonings for taste.

14. **Akara** - fried beans cake.

15. **Babalawo** – herbalist, faith diviner, ones who communicate with IFA for spiritual consultations.

16. **IFA** - Indigenous Faith of Africa (divination system that teaches the teaching of Orisha; Yoruba religion practices).

17. **Voodoo**(s) - black religious cult; a molded idol that is believed to possess spiritual powers/characterized by sorcery.

18. **Human ritual** - the practice of killing humans and harvesting body parts (head, organs, kidneys, hearts, etc.…) and offering them to the gods/herbalists to generate wealth and power.

19. **Indomies noodles -** instant noodles popularly eaten among young people.

20. **Ilu-oyinbo** - whites man land/abroad. Ilu- means country while oyinbo means, white man.

21. **Omo mi, bawo ni** - my child, how are you?

22. **Ogbono seeds/soup -** Nigerian soup, slimy in taste. And it contains assorted meat and fish.

ABOUT THE AUTHOR

Sade Eniola- author of *Escaping the Protectors*

Sade Eniola was born and raised in Nigeria but grew up in America. The main character Dami and the author could relate in so many ways, most especially growing up in the same country and culture. Growing up in America and while in school, Sade Eniola, volunteer at a Homeless shelter. Her exposure to the suffering of children around her age group, and vulnerable women and men touched her. Through her discussions with the group, she was amazed by how much impact she had in their lives; captivating and empowering each individual.

From this experience, Sade Eniola realized her desire in helping the underprivileged. She dedicated most of her life rendering help to those who are in need. In the group discussion, she was able to educate the group about the value of hope and perseverance, because she also grew up in a poor community. She understood how it feels to not have the basic necessity of life: Shelter, Food, and Love. Her passion in life is to empower her readers to dream big and to pursue their dreams no matter their background, socioeconomic status, or how ridiculous the dream may seem. If you dream it, it can be achieved, but first, there has to be a motivation. What is the driving force? She would ask.

After hearing Damilola Adeleke story, she was moved and emboldened. The story of Dami inspire the author to write. Through her writing, she hopes and believe she could encourage others; both young and old to open up and not to be defined by their past. Sade Eniola also wants to motivate her readers to stand up for the helpless. *Escaping the Protectors* is Sade Eniola first novel.